Memories of
Buddy Holly

Compiled by
Jim Dawson and Spencer Leigh

BIG NICKEL PUBLICATIONS
Post Office Box 157
Milford, New Hampshire 03055

Copyright 1996 by Jim Dawson and Spencer Leigh. No part of this publication may be copied or reproduced, stored in any retrieval system, or transmitted, in any form or by any means, electronic, mechanical, photocopying, recording, or otherwise, without prior written permission of Big Nickel Publications.

ISBN 0-936433-20-5. First printing September 1996. Printed in the U.S.A.

Special thanks to Bill Griggs, John Goldrosen, John Beecher and the late Malcolm Jones, without whom the legacy of Buddy Holly would be much less known to the world. Also thanks to Dick Blackburn, Steve Bonner, William J. Bush, Trevor Cajiao and the folks at *Now Dig This*, Rick Coleman, Andrew Doble, Neil Haislop, Jurgen Koop, Kathy Lownds-Reynolds, Ronnie Mack, Andy McKaie at MCA Records, Bobby "Fats" Mizzell, Peter Palombi, Jon Philibert, Steve Propes, Jeff Riley, BBC Radio Merseyside, and the many people who contributed quotes, comments and memories for this book.

Anyone looking for free information about publications and collectibles pertaining to Buddy Holly should write to Bill Griggs, c/o *Rockin' 50s* magazine, P.O. Box 6123, Lubbock, Texas 79493.

Table of Contents

Memories of Buddy Holly

1. Introduction: Why Are We Still Listening To This Guy?
   by Jim Dawson 5

2. "Memories Will Follow Me Forever...."
   a. "I'm Just Sittin' Here Reminiscing" 11
   b. "That'll Be The Day...." 87
   c. "Not Fade Away" 95

3. "Everyday, It's A-Gettin' Closer": 30 Important Dates In
   Buddy Holly's Life 119

4. "Listen To Me": Buddy Holly's Singles And Albums Released During
   His Lifetime 121

5. "Yeah, I'm Gonna Make Those Bells Ring": Buddy Holly's
   Chart Hits 123

6. "Changing All Those Changes": The Unreleased Buddy Holly
   Album Of Alternate Takes You Probably Haven't Heard 125

7. "Like A Talent Scout You Want Some Love That's New": Cover
   Records & Remakes Of Buddy Holly Songs 127

8. "Your Love For Me Has Got To Be Real": Paeans, Dirges And Tribute
   Records 143

9. "I Feel Like An Actor In A Play, Who Doesn't Fit The Part": Buddy
   Holly's Fictional Life 153

10. "When Someday You'll Want Me, I'll Be There, Wait And See":
    Buddy Holly Current CD Releases 157

11. Bibliography 163

12. The Compilers 167

COURTESY SHOWTIME ARCHIVES

One

Introduction
Why Are We Still Listening To This Guy?

By Jim Dawson

In August 1957, Buddy Holly's first hit record entered the charts. A year and a half later he was dead. Only three of his singles reached the Top 10 in America, and they were all released in 1957. By the time his plane crashed on February 3, 1959, Buddy was struggling to crack even the Top 40. In the news reports of the tragedy, he didn't even get top billing; Ritchie Valens was the only entertainer on that plane with a current hit. Buddy's death seemed to have merely hastened the plunge of a declining career.

Yet here we are, thirty-seven years later, and Buddy Holly's musical legend and legacy are more robust than ever. Jimi Hendrix could have been thinking of Buddy when he said, "Once you're dead, you're made for life." Buddy's death at age 22 turned out to be a brilliant career move. He never had a chance to record a Twist song, turn up in a cheesy movie, wear bellbottom trousers, play Vegas or Woodstock, sit enraptured at the feet of a guru, gain forty pounds, grow his hair long enough to look like his mother, wear a bad rug, write a rock opera, form a supergroup, leave his wife for a supermodel, use the lyric "turn on your love light," spend two weeks in the studio on one guitar solo, wear really big funny glasses, sing another Paul Anka song, cohost *The 700 Club*, shill Dick Clark's mail-order oldies on late-night cable TV, try to save the rain forests, hang out at fashion shows in Milan with Giorgio Armani, record with Third World jazz musicians nobody ever heard of, build a Holly Woods hillbilly theme park and pavilion just down the road from Twitty City, get a well-publicized liver transplant, ask Jeff Lynne to produce a comeback album, choke on his own vomit, or sing a duet with Loretta Lynn, Garth Brooks or Frank Sinatra.

Not that he would have done any of those things, but we'll never know. Like James Dean, Buddy is a pristine '50s figure, locked in amber, untarnished by the excesses and self-consciousness that overtook rock 'n' roll and other forms of American popular music by the mid-'60s. He'll never grow old or be anything but the carefree young guy wearing a V-neck sweater, horn-rims and a sunburst Fender Stratocaster slung over his shoulder, smiling out of the black-and-white photographs that comprise the bulk of what survives as his visual record. (On film there are only a few grainy kinescopes and some washed-out 8mm home movies.) For those of us growing up in the '50s, Buddy stayed behind in the glow of our youth and remains as that part of us. For those who heard him later, he's a tuneful ghost resurrected from the fading moments of American innocence.

Buddy's memory has probably been helped along by his select group of fans. As a skinny, four-eyed nerd who made good as a rocker, he was a beacon to those introverted, skinny, four-eyed boys who grew up to be writers, rock critics and rock performers themselves. Many years later, geeky, gawky, bespectacled Elvis Costello—often visually compared with Buddy Holly—would be accused of being a darling of rock critics precisely because he looked like them.

But rock 'n' rollers have to do more than simply look vulnerable or die young to become legends and cult icons. They have to create transcendental rock 'n' roll records that touch people's hearts, change the course of music, and remain fresh even after new courses have been charted by their musical descendants. Hendrix qualifies. So does Holly.

And so he's still with us in countless tangible forms. Somewhere right now an oldies radio station is broadcasting his voice and luminescent guitar work. His albums and CDs are selling steadily all over the world. His recordings regularly pop up in films (*American Graffiti, American Hot Wax, Peggy Sue Got Married, Stand By Me, Christine*). The surviving kinescopes of his live appearances on *The Arthur Murray Show* (hiccuping "Peggy Sue") and *The Ed Sullivan Show* (performing "That'll Be the Day" and "Peggy Sue" in early December 1957, and "Oh, Boy!" two months later) have been included in a dozen rock 'n' roll documentaries.

His songs have been recorded by hundreds of artists of every stripe—Esquerita, the Grateful Dead, Andy Williams, the Beatles, Kitty Kallen, John Denver, Phil Ochs, Blondie, the Stray Cats, the Rolling Stones, James Taylor, Sandy Denny, Link Wray, Linda Ronstadt, Nancy Griffith, Eric Clapton, The Band, Mary Chapin Carpenter, and the Everly Brothers, to name only a few. Buddy's songs are also catchy enough to be jingles in TV commercials—for Buick ("Oh, Buick!"), Toyota, and various cleaners and toiletries ("It's So Easy" being a perfect prescription for any household product; "Everyday" the rate of application to your furniture...or your teeth).

Several biographies have been published, including *Buddy Holly* (Collier Books, 1971) by Dave Laing, *Buddy Holly: A Biography in Words, Photographs and Music* (Peer International Corp., 1972) by Elizabeth and Ralph Peer, *Buddy Holly: His Life and Music* (Bowling Green University Popular Press, 1975) by John Goldrosen, *The Buddy Holly Story* (Quick Fox Books, 1979) by John Goldrosen, *The Buddy Holly Story* (Plexus, 1979) by John Tobler, *Remembering Buddy* (Penguin, 1986) by John Goldrosen and John Beecher, and *Buddy Holly: A Biography* (St. Martins

Press, 1995) by Ellis Amburn.

He was one of the first ten artists inducted into the Rock and Roll Hall of Fame in 1986.

He was the subject of a popular 1978 film, *The Buddy Holly Story*. Gary Busey, the actor who portrayed him, was nominated for an Academy Award for Best Actor. Musical director Joe Renzetti, using Buddy's songs, won an Oscar for Original Song Score and Its Adaptation or Adaptation Score.

Buddy also made an appearance (in the form of singer Marshall Crenshaw) in the 1987 Ritchie Valens film bio, *La Bamba*. A waiter impersonated Buddy in a '50s theme restaurant in director Quentin Tarantino's 1994 sensation, *Pulp Fiction*. And Buddy's name was invoked in *The Rocky Horror Picture Show* ("Whatever happened to Saturday night...Buddy Holly was singing, his very last song, with your arm around your girl, you tried to sing along") and in the 1973 classic, *American Graffiti*, when actor Paul LaMotte groused, "I can't stand that surfin' shit. Rock 'n' roll's been going downhill ever since Buddy Holly died!"

A stage play, *Buddy*, has been a hit in London's West End since 1989, played for a season at the Shubert Theater on Broadway, and toured North America in the early '90s.

Several documentaries have been made of Buddy's life, including Douglas Brooker's 1979 *Reminiscing* for Iowa Public Broadcasting, Paul McCartney's 1987 *The Real Buddy Holly Story*, which has aired all over the world (including the U.S., on PBS), and the U.K.'s Channel 4's 1996 hour-long film called *Not Fade Away*.

He has been the subject of a dozen tribute albums by the Hollies, Skeeter Davis, Bobby Vee, Jimmy Gilmer, Connie Francis and others; a recent tribute CD is *Not Fade Away*, recorded by several Nashville stars for MCA Records in late 1995 and lavishly hyped with film clips and interviews on The Nashville Network.

In 1993, Buddy's likeness appeared on a 29-cent U.S. postage stamp (five years after it debuted on a West German 50-pfennig stamp).

Buddy has cameoed as a fictional character in Robert B. Parker's *A Catskill Eagle* (as an intelligence agent who looks like him), in P.F. Kluge's *Eddie and the Cruisers* (at a secret 1958 recording session), and in George R.R. Martin's *Wild Cards* book series (as a has-been singing Prince and Bon Jovi songs at a Holiday Inn in an alternate universe). He also stars in Bradley Denton's 1991 Campbell Award-winning science fiction novel, *Buddy Holly Is Alive and Well on Ganymede* (as an alien on Jupiter's largest moon, jamming television all over the earth with his own rock videos). We've included excerpts in the section entitled "I Feel Like An Actor In A Play."

A Buddy Holly clone has been hiccupping at Legends in Concert at the Imperial Palace in Las Vegas for the past ten years.

In late 1989, when the Berlin Wall came down and the Communist world suddenly opened up to the Western media, a political cartoon from England's *Punch* magazine was syndicated all over the United States, showing a bearded prisoner breaking into the cell next to him to announce, "Buddy Holly's dead. Pass it on."

He was the spirit of a 1995 record, "Buddy Holly," by an alternative rock band called Weezer; the song charted in the Top 10 and won two major MTV awards.

Every September, Great Britain celebrates his birthday with Buddy Holly Week and his hometown, Lubbock, Texas, sponsors a Buddy Holly concert with major artists. Every February the cavernous Surf Ballroom in Clear Lake, Iowa, where he performed his last show, salutes Buddy Holly with a concert that attracts thousands of people from all over the world. The Surf, incidentally, is located these days on a road called Buddy Holly Place.

A reissue of his hits, *Buddy Holly Lives: 20 Golden Greats*, went to number one on the German and British album charts in 1978. Another Buddy Holly anthology, *Words of Love*, reached the top of Britain's charts in early 1993.

When an IRA bomb destroyed a bus in the middle of London on February 20, 1996, a photo of the charred wreckage was beamed to newspapers and magazines all around the world, showing that all that survived the carnage was a large advertisement on its side for the play *Buddy*.

Buddy Holly! The name has the same mellifluous magic as his music. No one else looked like him, wrote songs like him, or sang and played guitar like him. As the passing years telescope old celebrities and once-important events into the blur of history, he remains a clear human symbol of a time and a music.

The cultist conspiracy nuts who think Buddy survived that 1959 plane crash have it partially right. He may not be living as a vegetable in a Caribbean hideaway or in the catacombs of the Vatican, but Buddy Holly lives on, nonetheless.

Buddy's Birthplace
Photo: Jim Dawson

Buddy at age 13 (above), and at age 6 (lower left)
Photos: Showtime Archives

Buddy's class photo, 1955
Photo: Ralph Dewitt Photo/
Bill Griggs Collection

Buddy, 1953 (above), and with his first girlfriend Echo McGuire, 1955 (right)
Photos: Bill Griggs Collection

Two
"Memories Will Follow Me Forever..."
"I'm Just Sittin' Here Reminiscing"

BUDDY HOLLY (Writing an English assignment during his sophomore year, early 1953.)
I was born one fall day, a certain particular one, because it was September 7, 1936, and school for that year was starting. It also [was] the first Monday of the month and Dollar Day, and also Labor Day, so you see, it was very eventful in more ways than one. Mr. and Mrs. L. O. Holley were the happy parents of this bouncing, baby boy, or so I'm told, because I was a little young then to be remembering it now.

ELLA HOLLEY (Buddy's mother.)
Charles Hardin Holley was too long a name for such a little boy, so we called him Buddy.

LARRY HOLLEY (Buddy's eldest brother.)
Well, he made his presence known right from the start and we all sorta spoiled him, because he was so much younger than the rest of us.

TRAVIS HOLLEY (Buddy's older brother.)
I had played accordion for years, but a shipmate of mine named Jesse Issom from Jonesboro, Arkansas, got me interested in guitar when we were in Hawaii, right after Iwo Jima. By the time I got home, I knew a few chords, and Buddy started bugging me to teach him how to play.

ELLA HOLLEY
Larry and Travis already played a couple of instruments, and I thought it was about time Buddy learned to play something too.

BUDDY HOLLY (In an interview for England's *New Musical Express* in 1958.)
I first started playing guitar when I was in the seventh grade at junior high school back home in Lubbock. It cost me around $45, and I taught myself to play.

LARRY HOLLEY
Hank Williams was out on "Lovesick Blues" and one day we heard Buddy singing this song. He did a pretty good job on it, even though his voice was still pretty high. He got a guitar and started messing around with it.

JACK NEAL (Buddy's first singing partner in 1952 and cowriter of Buddy's second record, "Modern Don Juan.")
I played rhythm, Buddy played lead... We'd go out to these black cafes on the other side of the tracks and just sit and listen. They mostly served barbecue, which we liked. He'd say, "Jack, I don't want to be rich. I don't even want to be in the

limelight. But I want people to remember the name Buddy Holly."

BUDDY HOLLY (In a hand-printed letter written about 1953-54, soliciting work.)
We are a group of high-school boys that has organized one of the leading hill-billy & Western bands in Lubbock. We are interested in helping neighborhood high schools to raise funds and at the same time raise money for us to help pay our way through high school.
  I know that you wouldn't want to let just anyone play at your school, so if you have not heard of us, we are the 580 Ranch Hands & Buddy and Jack, and we have two radio programs every Sunday afternoon at 3:15 o'clock and 3:30 o'clock respectively. The radio station we are on, is KDAV (580 on your radio dial). If it would not be asking too much, we would like to request your listening to our programs and see if you like us. If you need any references, you may write to Hi-Pockets, or Dave Stone c/o radio station KDAV here in Lubbock, and ask them about us. Now, here is what we would like to ask you about. We would like to come to your school and play a stage show for the entertainment of the citizens, school-children, and neighboring farms people of your town. We could advertise over the radio when we were going to be there and get a good audience built up. I know that if your school is like our school, it can always use some extra money. We have helped quite a few schools around Austin, Texas, to gather money in this way and they were quite satisfied with the results. If you are at all interested in this, we would appreciate it very much if you would write to me, Buddy Holley, 2304-1st Street, Lubbock, Texas.

BOB MONTGOMERY (Buddy's first recording partner, half of *The Buddy & Bob Show* on radio.)
We loved bluegrass, and we were trying to pattern ourselves after people like Flatt & Scruggs, Bill Monroe, the Louvin Brothers... We'd try to pick up licks from the records, and a lot of those guys would come through Lubbock and we'd watch them very closely during their shows.

DAVE STONE (Owner of Lubbock radio station KDAV, home of *The Buddy & Bob Show*.)
They were hits almost immediately from the time they went on. Believe me, they didn't any more than get that show started when the phone would start ringing off the hook.

LARRY WELBORN (Lubbock musician.)
I was playing a little place called Tommy's Danceland over in East Lubbock. I wasn't supposed to be there, I was under-age, and Buddy came out and just started talking to me. He was wanting me to play bass, he and Bob were together then, and he wanted me to play slap bass. I had played bass before, so I started doing that... We used to play all the car lots and supermarkets and stuff like that.

Buddy sitting in with hillbilly band.
Borger, TX, 1954

Grocery store opening, 1955
L to R: Hi-pockets, Buddy, L. Welborn

(left) Buddy and Bob with L. Welborn on base at park, 1955.

Photos: Bill Griggs Collection

Buddy, 1956
Photo: Showtime Archives

GEORGE ATWOOD (Lubbock musician.)
Buddy, Bob and Larry played a mixture of bluegrass and middle-of-the-road country. I knew Larry, Bob and Waylon Jennings before I met Buddy. They were playing at the openings of car dealers, grocery stores, dances and private parties, and were already writing some of their own material.

SONNY CURTIS (Lubbock-based musician who played guitar on Buddy's first sessions.)
When Bob learned that I played fiddle, he said, "Wait, we've got to go right over to Buddy Holly's place." It seemed like we'd been playing together for years, everything just fell right into place. I remember Buddy was playing a four-string banjo, which kind of turned him off because [Earl] Scruggs had a 5-string, but he made it sound just as good as Earl's. I was definitely impressed.

BOB MONTGOMERY
He was quite versatile, you know. He could play banjo, mandolin and he had a great rhythm, really wailing on this old Epiphone guitar that he had. When we started playing electric, around 1954, he'd play whatever lead there was to our songs. Primarily, though, we both just flat-picked rhythm. I concentrated on singing melody and Buddy sang harmony.

SONNY CURTIS
Then along came Little Richard, Fats Domino, Ray Charles—he was a little more sophisticated, we couldn't figure out some of his chords—and of course Chuck Berry. At the outset, we couldn't listen to that music 'cause it was considered race music. We'd have to go out in the car late at night and listen to this show [on KWKH] out of Shreveport, Louisiana, which played the greatest music in the world. I used to spend the night with Holly, we'd go out at midnight and sit in his car, and fall asleep listening to the music.

BOB MONTGOMERY
We had been interested in Hank Williams because he had a kind of blues feeling to his music. But listen-

ing to Shreveport exposed us to people like Muddy Waters, Howlin' Wolf, Little Walter. So we just started incorporating more blues into our act.

ELLA HOLLEY
I liked the sort of music he was listening to. Especially those black gospel singers—some of those songs were so pretty. He liked Ray Charles a lot.

NIKI SULLIVAN (Buddy's rhythm guitarist in the Crickets.)
Lubbock is so isolated, your options are really limited. You either work at Texas Tech, get into cotton farming, or find some trade—like music— that'll carry you elsewhere. That's why Lubbock has so many good musicians.

JERRY ALLISON (Buddy's closest friend and drummer.)
I met him in J.T. Hutchinson Junior High School. I was probably in the seventh grade then. I didn't know he played at all. I didn't know about him playing until he played at school. He and Bob Montgomery were singing "Too Old to Cut the Mustard," which is quite a country tune.

WILLIAM "HI-POCKETS" DUNCAN (Buddy & Bob's manager.)
I could see right away that Buddy had it, a lot of grit, a lot of determination—he just had more drive than the other youngsters there.

BUDDY HOLLY
Without Elvis, none of us would have made it.

SONNY CURTIS
We had heard Elvis of course on those lovely Sun records, and he came to Lubbock when we were still in high school, and we played on that show. The next day we became Elvis clones. I had a D-28 Martin and Buddy had a Fender Stratocaster. Buddy took my Martin and I took his Strat and he was like Elvis and I was like Scotty Moore.

HI-POCKETS DUNCAN
Between sets that night [in January 1955 at Lubbock's Cotton Club], Elvis just sat in a corner, drinking a Coke. And Buddy and Bob were there that

Young Elvis
Photo: Jim Dawson

night—I don't know what the age limits were there, but they came down all the time to see the shows. And so they went over to talk to Elvis. Later Buddy said to me, "You know, he's a real nice, friendly fellow."...Elvis was enough of a star to be paid to play at the grand opening of the local Pontiac dealership the next day. Buddy and his trio played there, too. And when the next KDAV *Sunday Party* rolled around, Buddy was singing Elvis's songs.

DAVE STONE
The boys talked with Elvis for a long time. They decided to change their style. The next week I was announcing the show and my wife was answering the phones, when, without our knowing about it, the boys started their new sound. Where there had been little interest before, suddenly the phone rang off the wall. It wasn't exactly Presley's style, it was something in their own vein.

SONNY CURTIS
Presley just blew Buddy away. None of us had ever seen anything like Elvis, the way he could get the girls jumping up and down, and that definitely impressed Holly. But it was the music that really turned Buddy around... After seeing Elvis, Buddy had only one way to go.

WAYLON JENNINGS (Lubbock disc jockey who later recorded and toured with Buddy.)
I saw Elvis Presley in 1955, I guess it was, in Lubbock. Well, it changed things in a way. I think it changed Buddy, too; at least I think it had a bearing. Actually it changed almost everything, really.

BUDDY HOLLY (Talking with deejay Pat Barton in Australia, January 31, 1958.)
I used to know Elvis quite well before he got as popular as he is now.

NORMAN PETTY (Buddy's record producer on his Brunswick and Coral recordings.)
I think he really appreciated Elvis and I'm sure Elvis was an influence on him as he was on so many others, but I really think that Buddy was a broader artist than that, to the extent that Buddy appreciated anybody who was talented. He thought Ray Charles was sensational. He thought Bo Diddley was great.

LARRY WELBORN
I was with Elvis a lot at that time. Buddy was too. In fact, we'd go to Elvis's motel room when he and Scotty Moore and Bill Black...were coming down here [to Lubbock]. There weren't that many musicians around at that time, so when they came into town, we'd go to their motel room and gab with them, then go do the show.

JERRY ALLISON
The second time Elvis came to town, he and Buddy hung out and went to the movies. Buddy taught Elvis the words to [Clyde McPhatter & the Drifters'] "Money Honey," and Elvis cut it right after that.

LARRY WELBORN
We really got into the rockabilly thing. We still did a lot of the country things like Johnny and Jack's "Poison Love" and stuff like that. We'd also do stuff like "Ooby Dooby" by Roy Orbison... And "Annie Had a Baby" and things like that.

ROY ORBISON (West Texas country and rockabilly singer.)
I would go to see Buddy's shows and he would go to see mine, back and forth there. Buddy was a very bright boy, very dedicated. He wasn't uppity, or as we'd say in the business, "flashy." He could tell jokes. We had a relationship that developed.

JERRY ALLISON
We listened to a lot of rhythm and blues records which have a lot of horn rides in them. Unfortunately, we didn't have any horn players, so we'd try to imitate the overall sound of the record—the horn rides and all—with just the guitar and drums....Buddy would imitate the saxophone with down strokes on his guitar, and I'd play the same rhythm lick on the snare. It wasn't really like a horn section, but it was close enough to catch the feel of the record.

PEGGY SUE GERRON (Jerry Allison's girlfriend, later wife; inspired the song title "Peggy Sue.")
The way Buddy played guitar, they always "spoke" to each other, between the drums and the guitar. If Buddy had a guitar riff, then Jerry would have one which would stick to it. They communicated with the music.

JERRY ALLISON
We'd play for 45 minutes, take a 15-minute break and then play some more. We repeated a few tunes, but we knew a lot of songs. We did Little Richard songs and instrumentals like "Honky Tonk." We once played for five hours at a dance and we started writing songs so that we would have more songs to play.

SONNY CURTIS
If there was a lick on any record, Buddy could nail it immediately. He could do just about anything he wanted on guitar, but he only played what he felt he needed.

JERRY ALLISON
If you said, "All right: Play an E-major-7th-diminished-double-clutch-in-Eb," he probably wouldn't know what you were talking about, but he could play it. He knew what he wanted to get out of a guitar, and he didn't go a step further.

NIKI SULLIVAN
Buddy's style of playing the guitar was a rhythm style where you were playing all six strings all the time, where most guitarists only played one or two strings in their work.

JERRY ALLISON
There was a little colored beer joint just outside of [San Angelo]. We were hungry and wanted some hamburgers, so we went in and sat down.

They had a three-piece colored band playing. Buddy went up and started talking to them, and they knew from how he talked that he was a musician. One of them said, "Hey, man, why don't you play one!" Buddy said, "Don't mind if I do." He picked up that electric guitar, and as soon as he touched it, the sound was completely different. He played "Sexy Ways," and everybody looked up. Somebody made a phone call and people started coming in, and it wasn't long until that place was packed.

SID KING (Leader of a popular country-rockabilly band.)
We were regulars on the *Big D Jamboree* [broadcasting over KRLD in Dallas], so one time I said, "Well, Buddy, why don't you come on up, and we'll get you on the *Jamboree*." And we must have told him what week we'd be on, 'cause we didn't play every Saturday, we only worked there once a month. Well, you couldn't say something like that to Buddy, 'cause he'd be there the next day. And that's kind of what happened—he didn't even call us or anything, he just showed up, him and the others. He came in on Friday night and he spent the night in my house. And so I introduced him to Johnny Harper, who was the talent coordinator on the *Jamboree*, and they put Buddy on the show that night. He did two or three songs, and I think he encored.

LARRY WELBORN
I don't think he was stuck-up, he was more confident than anything else.

He had the attitude: If they can do it, I can do it, and that was just it. You couldn't run him down, there was no question in his mind that he was going to do it.

ELLA HOLLEY
We were against drinking alcohol or smoking cigarettes, and Buddy didn't hold to that strictly. When he started smoking, he'd do it on the sly, thinking I didn't know, and finally I said, "If you're going to smoke, don't bother hiding it, just come out here in the living room and do it here." He drank, but not too much; at least I can only remember him being drunk once.

LARRY HOLLEY
He wasn't no saint by any means. He certainly wasn't a goody-goody. He was a saint in the fact that he was a saved Christian. He accepted Christ as his savior when he was younger.

SONNY CURTIS
Though in appearance Buddy was very neat and always wore tapered jeans, he was not shy. He was a drinker—loud, a smart aleck, headstrong.

LARRY HOLLEY
This was a very jealous town and there was always some guys that wanted to beat up on him because he was popular with some of their girlfriends. They'd make remarks. There was a lot of jealousy among Texas boys against anybody in their area that is famous or drawing some

attention. That's just the way Texans are. There were a few times that me and Travis had to go to the roller rink and see if Buddy was getting into trouble.

BUDDY HOLLY
If people are going to like me, they'll just have to like me with my glasses on.

DR. J. DAVIS ARMISTEAD (Buddy's optician in Lubbock.)
He had a severe stigmatism. As for his eyesight, I'd have to check his records. [Buddy was 20/800 in each eye.]

JERRY ALLISON
We did [a show] for the Pontiac house over on Avenue Q, I think it was Quinn Connelly Pontiac. We also did a Furr Food Store opening. We'd be on the back of a semi truck at 34th and Avenue H... We played for a Humble service station in Slaton for a guy named Crest or something like that. We'd play an opening for the price of a pack of cigarettes in those days.

SONNY CURTIS
We played a club in Lubbock that was a bit questionable. It was a teenage club and they did the dirty bop there. It was an extension of a dance called the bop, and you can figure out the rest of it. The local newspaper took pictures of us playing there with the kids doing the dirty bop, and they put the picture in the paper with our eyes blacked out.

EDDIE CRANDALL (Nashville talent scout, in a telegram to KDAV's Dave Stone in late 1955.)
Dave, I'm very confident I can do something as far as getting Buddy Holly a recording contract. It may not be a major, but even a small one would be beneficial to someone who is trying to get a break. And he's got to start somewhere. Anyway, I'll see what I can do... Marty Robbins also thinks Buddy has what it takes. So, all we can do is try.

NORMAN PETTY
Clovis is in New Mexico, a little town of about 35,000 people, and it's about 100 miles from Lubbock, Texas, and Buddy and Bob had their center of operations in Lubbock... I didn't become involved with Buddy until 1956. At that time he came over and recorded some demos [at my studio], but even then most of those early demos were recorded by the boys at home. At the time I met Buddy and Bob they were on the point of splitting up because Bob wanted to stay with country music and Buddy wanted to move into rock 'n' roll... He came in and said, "If you can get Buddy Knox a hit, you can get me a hit." I thought that was pretty remarkable and I told him then that it was not the place, it was the artist. So he recorded his demos, took them to Nashville and actually landed his first record deal himself.

LARRY HOLLEY
Buddy came to me and asked me for

a loan so he could buy a new guitar and amplifiers... I asked him how much he needed, and he said a thousand dollars. I didn't mind giving him that much, but I wondered if it was wise to spend money that way—I think six hundred dollars went for the guitar alone... That was when he bought that Fender Stratocaster, the one he used on all his records and in his concerts.

SONNY CURTIS
Buddy bought a Stratocaster way before the Crickets. I don't know why he bought one, and don't know if it was a vision or what... I wouldn't have bought one myself because it was a sort of futuristic-looking thing and I would have been scared of it... You could turn that thing up where you could blow the back end out of a building and it wouldn't feed back on you, and of course we liked that because we loved to play loud.

BUDDY HOLLY (Writing to Decca executive Paul Cohen in early 1956.)
My junior year my singing pardner [sic] and I started singing on radio station KDAV on Sunday evenings. Soon after this I started singing semi-professionally. Eddie Crandall heard me sing a show with Bill Haley in November of 1955. He asked me to send you some dubs in Nashville. Soon after I was notified that I would have a session.

SONNY CURTIS
As I remember, we left for Nashville in a bit of a hurry. Buddy was driving a new 1955 Oldsmobile then; his family had traded in their old car and sort of given him this new one as a graduation present, but he was supposed to make the payments on it. So he was trying to stay one step ahead of the collection agency, and I think that's why we left so quick. There was Don Guess and Buddy and me.

JERRY ALLISON
Someone [at Decca] signed Buddy to do rock 'n' roll, and when he got there, someone didn't have the same frame of mind that the one who signed him did.

SONNY CURTIS
I don't think anybody there was really very interested in Buddy. I don't think they thought about him being a big star, or wanted him to go in any particular direction. They just made a contract and were going to record him. Best I remember, nobody messed with us at all, or told us how they wanted it to sound—they just turned on the mikes and let us go. They weren't really into rock 'n' roll, and they didn't know what to do.

BEN HALL (Composer of Buddy's first record, "Blue Days, Black Nights.")
["Blues Days, Black Nights"] was not recorded the way that Buddy had wanted it, and not the way I thought it should be either. The recording was done in Nashville, Tennessee, and they did not understand what Buddy was trying to do.

JERRY ALLISON
We didn't have an upright bass, and we were told by the producer [Owen Bradley] to get a bass in 30 minutes or he was going water skiing. That's how interested he was. We borrowed a fellow's bass and recorded it.

OWEN BRADLEY
We had been very successful with a country formula; we were all into country, and it's hard to change patterns. Buddy couldn't fit into our formula any more than we could fit into his... Buddy was trying to make sort of a rock 'n' roll record, and he should have had guys with a black feel—our guys had a country feel.

JERRY ALLISON
I really can't remember what Buddy thought about "Blue Days, Black Nights" and those things—at the time he was pretty tickled just to have a record out and he took it around to the radio stations and said, "Hey, listen to this."

BILL PICKERING
I was a disc jockey at KLLL radio on the 20th floor of the Great Plains Life Building, right here in Lubbock. I was sitting in the studio one day doing my show and the door opened. A young man stepped inside. He was wearing blue jeans, a white T-shirt, and he had a patch on the knee of his blue jeans. He was holding a record closely to his side... He asked, "Could I get you to play my record?" I said, "Well, let's see. Let me play this other one, then we'll put yours on the turntable and audition it and see how it sounds." He said okay, so we did that, and I listened to a little bit of it and liked it... I finished playing the record that I was playing, gave the time, and as I already had his record on the turntable, I said into the microphone, "We have a young man in the studio with us, a guest, who has a record that we're going to play in just a moment, but first, I'm going to interview him on the air." I turned to him and said, "Young man, would you give us your name?" He bent over near the microphone and said, "I'm Buddy Holly." I said, "All right, Buddy, where did you record this record?" He said, "Nashville." I said, "Fine, I want you to bend over here near the microphone and introduce this record." He said, "All right, ladies and gentlemen, this is Buddy Holly singing 'Blue Days, Black Nights.'"

BILLBOARD MAGAZINE (April 21, 1956)
Blue Days-Black Nights....77
DECCA 29854—Warbler, tune, guitar, etc., are patterned very closely after Elvis Presley. Good material and production on both sides. Should do fine.
Love Me.....80
Cedarwood succumbs to rock and roll, too. If the public will take more than one Presley or Perkins, as it well may, Holly stands a strong chance.

ROY ORBISON
"Blue Days, Black Nights" sounded just like Elvis. Buddy followed Elvis and they were both tied up in my thinking.

Buddy recording in Nashville, 1956
Photo: Jim Dawson

Gene Vincent
Photo: Jim Dawson

GENE VINCENT (Early rockabilly star whose "Be-Bop-A-Lula" was a 1956 hit.)
I went back to the hotel [in Nashville] and there was this fella sitting there in the lobby who came up to me and said, "Excuse me, can I get your autograph?" and I said, "Haven't I seen you someplace before?" and he said, "Yeah, my name's Buddy Holly." He had a record out then called "Blue Days, Black Nights." It was a fabulous record.

THE LUBBOCK JOURNAL, October 23, 1956 (written by staff writer Mary Lou Fairbairn)
Lubbock now has its own "answer to Elvis Presley." He is Buddy Holly, 20-year-old graduate of Lubbock High School, who recently signed a five-year contract with Decca Recording Co., and who is "packing them in" on weekends at the American Legion Youth Center.

Holly, who has "a three-piece orchestra just like Presley's," has reverted to playing and singing rock 'n' roll exclusively. He plays an electric standard guitar and wears "fancy" sports coats for his singing engagements, but the resemblance to the widely known entertainer ends there. Holly refuses to wear one of the bright sports coats on the street, even for publicity.

Holly had two numbers released by Decca in May—"Blue Days, Black Nights" and "Love Me"—and by the end of June 19,000 copies of the record had been sold. He was given a good mention of the first release in "Billboard Magazine."

The young Lubbock singer proved his versatility when he co-authored one of the first songs he recorded. He and Sue Parrish, a former Lubbock girl who now lives on the West Coast, wrote "Love Me." The other side of the record was written by Ben Hall, former Lubbock man now in Big Spring.

The record was made at Decca's recording headquarters in Nashville, Tenn., and Holly is to go there for another recording session in about two weeks.

Accompanying him for the first record were Don Guess, 19, bass player, and Jerry Allison, 17, drummer, both Lubbock High graduates, Sonny Curtis of Lubbock and Grady Martin of Nashville. Guess and Allison together with Holly playing the guitar, make up Holly's orchestra. Holly does not accompany himself as he sings for recording sessions, however.

The son of Mr. and Mrs. L.O. Holley, Rt. 5, he modestly says he also plays the banjo, mandolin and piano "a little." He says he began playing music at about age 13 and began professionally as a musician at 17. He has had his own band two years.

However, his father says Buddy has been playing "all his life" and is quite proud of a violin prize he won at age 5 and a first place he won in the annual Westerner Round-Up at Lubbock High.

His mother says he began violin lessons at 6, and also had lessons on the piano and Hawaiian steel guitar. He sang first tenor in the senior acappella choir at Lubbock High School, but says his voice has changed since then.

His first interest in music came from his older brothers, Larry and Travis, who played several instruments a few years ago. He now spends his spare time working with them in the Lubbock Ceramic Tile business they operate.

Versatile in fields other than music, Holly says his love after music is water skiing. He also loves motorcycle riding, reading and doing leather work.

He is becoming busier with his music, however, and his recording contract calls for new releases each of the next four years.

A booking agent has kept Holly and his orchestra fairly busy with one-night stands about 200 miles apart. While he has presented stage performances mostly, Holly takes a special interest in playing for the American Legion Youth Center, 2nd St. and College Ave., which had an attendance last Saturday of about 350 and is increasing attendance weekly. He also has toured with Grand Ole Opry shows.

DON GUESS
On our early tours, we were wide-eyed youngsters from Lubbock and the music business was just fantastic to us....We had Buddy's car, and we carried the bass fiddle right on top of it—and I remember, one of those guys that was touring with us, Faron Young, we pulled into some town in Florida, and he was out in the street, and he said, "Gee whiz, look at those hillbillies."

ELLA HOLLEY
I didn't always see that much of Buddy—he was always on the go, running around with his friends. But when he came in at night, I'd fix up some peanut butter and jelly sandwiches, and we'd sit in the kitchen and talk about things—we called it our jam session.

JERRY ALLISON
Buddy and Sonny Curtis and me saw *The Searchers* with John Wayne over at the State Theater on Texas Avenue. All through that movie John Wayne says, "That'll be the day." So about a day later we were practicing in my bedroom and Buddy said, "Let's write a song together," and I said, "That'll be the day." Buddy lit up and said,

"Yeah, that sounds like a good idea."

SONNY CURTIS
My dad's a farmer and we had a black man that helped us out called Willie Robertson. Willie's wife used to help my mom around the house sometimes—not on a full-time basis 'cause we couldn't afford a maid, but just occasionally to help out with the ironing or housecleaning. Her name was Ollie Vee, but beyond that it's just a name. "Rock Around With Ollie Vee" has nothing to do with her. I just used her name. I love Buddy's voice on that track—it's really nice. Grady Martin played rhythm, I played lead and Buddy didn't play anything at all.

JERRY ALLISON
The first time we recorded ["That'll Be the Day"] was in Nashville for Decca Records. It was the summer of '56 and I had just gotten out of school. The producer said, "That's the worst song I've ever heard in my life." That hurt my feelings 'cause it was the first song I'd written.

SONNY CURTIS
In Nashville there was sort of a formula for cutting records, and although we didn't necessarily agree with it, we didn't have an alternative in mind. We knew the sessions weren't quite what we wanted, but we didn't quite know how to go about it. For one thing, I think a mistake was made. Buddy was such a good guitarist and had such a great feel. He didn't even play [on many cuts]. He just stood at the mike and sang. I played the lead and Grady Martin, one of the great guitarists of all time, played rhythm on those dates. We also had a drummer, Buddy Harmon. He was fantastic. But it was sort of us and them. They just showed up to play the sessions, and we just could never get a feel for each other....Those sessions just didn't have the right feeling.

BILLBOARD (December 29, 1956)
Modern Don Juan.....79
DECCA 30166—This is patterned after the Presley medium tempo rhythm numbers. The material has a simple and appealing riff that is very much in the current teen-age groove. Will be appreciated by many.
You Are My One Desire....70
Holly quavers thru this ballad in a way that resembles the styling of Presley's "Love Me Tender." There's a sound here of arresting quality.

SONNY CURTIS
In those days we were so naive that we thought all we had to do was get a record out, and then it would be instant success. I remember seeing one of our songs reviewed in *Billboard* and saying, "Boy, we have arrived!" Needless to say, that wasn't the case.

PAUL COHEN (Decca's Nashville A&R man.)
Buddy Holly is the biggest no-talent I have ever worked with.

NORMAN PETTY
He was with them for about one year. He tried to get the Decca people to let him record in Clovis at my studio, and they just said, "Clovis, where?"

GEORGE ATWOOD
Clyde Hankins, an excellent guitar picker working around Lubbock, was doing some stuff for Norman Petty. Both of us had jazz backgrounds. I'd worked with Artie Shaw, the Dorseys, Gene Krupa. Anyway, Clyde wanted to do an album with me. We drove over to Clovis on a Sunday. While Clyde and I were cutting our first session, a young man walked in that I recognized from seeing him around Lubbock. He walked into the control room with Norman, and during the session Norman kept pointing me out.

A few minutes later Clyde and I took a break for a smoke and a cold drink. I went in to find out what was going on. Norman introduced the young man as Buddy Holly. Buddy asked me, "Would you mind doing some recording with me?" Norman asked if I'd like to do some studio work. Turned out that Clyde had taught Buddy how to play guitar early on, but Buddy didn't want to spend time on the old stuff we were playing. He wanted to move forward. I think Buddy had just been in Nashville a few days earlier and was very upset with Decca. I ended up playing bass on a lot of Buddy's recordings.

NORMAN PETTY
My first impression of [Buddy] was of a person ultra-eager to succeed… He wore a T-shirt and Levi's. Really, he was unimpressive to look at, but impressive to hear. In fact, businessmen around here asked me why I was interested in a hillbilly like Holly and I told them I thought Buddy was a diamond in the rough.

BUDDY KNOX (Texas rockabilly artist whose "Party Doll" was a number-one hit in 1957.)
Norman kind of let us slip through his fingers because he didn't realize we had two hit songs on our hands, and when Buddy Holly came through he got hold of Buddy and Buddy's management and booking—the whole works.

BUDDY HOLLY (Talking with disc jockey Freeman Hoover.)
We've known Norm for quite some time down in Clovis, New Mexico. We used to go over and make a few dubs now and then, to see what we sounded like and everything, so, the last time—oh, let's see, it was in January [1957] I believe… we went over there and we were making a dub to send in to various companies and see if we could possibly do anything in the line of the music business.

NORMAN PETTY
When I saw Buddy Holly perform, I knew that he was so fresh and intense and that he was sold on the idea he was going to be a hit artist, even way back then. I think that

determination and his lack of inhibition were what attracted me to him in the first place.

BUDDY KNOX
We tended to record [in Clovis] at eleven at night and go on till five in the morning, mainly because of Norman's echo chamber that was on top of his dad's garage next door. He had a speaker on one end of the roof and a microphone at the other end, and every time a truck passed by outside, it could be heard in the studio and we'd have to cut it again.

NORMAN PETTY
We were one of the first [studios] in the states to use Telefunken condenser microphones. The studio was not a country bumpkin operation. The only piece of equipment that was more technically advanced was the eight-track machine that Ampex had developed for Les Paul.

JERRY ALLISON
[Norman] was a great engineer and had excellent equipment and a good echo chamber. He knew which equipment worked better on what instrument. He knew his studio well, since he'd designed it. He knew where drums would sound better in the room.

SONNY CURTIS
I wasn't getting along with Holly that well—we sort of had a conflict of personality. But the main reason I quit was because we weren't making any money.

JERRY ALLISON
There wasn't really any steady group, it was just whatever came up and whoever was hanging around at the time and was available to play.

NIKI SULLIVAN
I didn't start as a Cricket until the end of 1956, November or December of that year. I had been awestruck by Elvis, he's the one who got me to pick up my guitar. And Buddy was the closest thing to Elvis that we had in Lubbock. So I made it a point to get introduced to him over at his house, and we started jamming together.

JERRY ALLISON
There had been a group called the Spiders with a record called "Witchcraft," and we said, "Hey, that's a good record, and we need a group name—insects, that's good." So we looked under insects and decided on Crickets because they made noise anyway.

BUDDY HOLLY (Talking with disc jockey Dale Lowry in Topeka, Kansas, November 5, 1957.)
We had to think of some name that hadn't been used yet, and Jerry came up with it, so sure enough it'd already been used [by a New York R&B vocal group], but it'd been a good while back so it didn't matter too much.

NORMAN PETTY
Once, in the studio, he did this little hiccuping thing, kind of like hiccup-

ing through the words. I think he did it to make me laugh in the control room. We left it on the record and soon everyone was imitating it.

CHARLIE FEATHERS (Memphis rockabilly artist who cowrote Elvis's "I Forgot to Remember to Forget.")
I've been singing rockabilly most of my life. Buddy Holly would go out and listen to me. He tried to get on Sun and then he went to Clovis, New Mexico... and a lot of people say we sound alike. He used to listen to me do the hiccup, so who copied who?

BUDDY HOLLY (Talking on the phone with Decca executive Paul Cohen, February 28, 1957, trying to get the rights to re-record "That'll Be the Day" for another label.)
Uh, I thought I'd call you about my, uh, contract [with Decca]. I noticed that it wasn't renewed and I just took it for granted that it was gonna be canceled... in December, you know, and so I thought if it would be all right with you that if, uh, I wondered if I could just go ahead and get my release and everything... Well, you remember those songs that we cut back in the summertime that never was released? I wondered if I could get a... get you to send me a release on them so we might could try to do something with them... Yes sir, but, I mean, the session was, you know, it was called off. I mean it wasn't released, it was taken as a bad session... those five songs we cut back in the summer... I know that you told me and Mr. Bradley told me that they would never release those 'cause they weren't any good... It seems sort of a heck of a way to do a guy... We was wanting to cut a master like you said, on our own, pay for it ourself, and see if we could sell it to somebody.

BUDDY KNOX
Buddy and myself and Roy Orbison had about the only three rock 'n' roll type bands in that whole part of the United States at the time, I guess, so it was inevitable that we would run across each other sooner or later. Then we met Buddy and the Crickets at a show sometime... I think Roy Orbison was playing. And then Buddy and the Crickets came up to my house and we sat down on the front porch all night long and just jammed—we played and sang and went through our songs, and he went through a thing he'd written with J.I. called "That'll Be the Day." I said, "Hey, that's really a good song, man." Then I went through "Party Doll," and he said, "Hey, that's a really good song." Anyway, from then on we were friends and when we got on the road together, we worked a lot of dates on the road up until 1959.

GARY TOLLETT (Recording artist who, with his wife Romona and cousin June Clark, sang background on "That'll Be the Day.")
We met and we would play for hours on end in the evenings at [June Clark's] house rehearsing different numbers. That's where "That'll Be the Day" got started, the new recording, the one that made the hit. Of course,

Buddy had "That'll Be the Day" prior to that time, but it wasn't the new version of it.

NORMAN PETTY
Whether it took 30 minutes or three hours, the price was the same. Then you had the time to create something nice and do it right.

JERRY ALLISON
In Clovis we did ["That'll Be the Day"] just like we'd been doing it onstage... We'd always wanted to get three black girls to sing [background] like the Raeletts of Ray Charles, that kind of sound.

GARY TOLLETT
Buddy helped me make some demo recordings. By him doing that for me without any charge, I felt that we certainly owed Buddy something. Buddy had asked Romona and I if we would help him record something by doing backup vocal work... So that was how "That'll Be the Day" came about. We worked on it at Nig and June Clark's house several times, and we rehearsed it at Norman Petty's studio in Clovis several times before we got what we felt was the right rendition.

TOMMY ALLSUP (Buddy's lead guitarist on most of his later recordings.) He played just about everything in A, to fit his vocal range. Even on "That'll Be the Day," that has an open E riff, Buddy would capo up to the 5th fret so that he could sing it in A.

JERRY ALLISON
He liked the way [bluesman] Lonnie Johnson played—that blues lick in "That'll Be the Day" probably comes from Lonnie's influence, an old song called "Jelly Roll."

LARRY WELBORN
That's my one claim to fame. I played [bass] on "That'll Be the Day" and nobody knows it.

GARY TOLLETT
We started recording about nine o'clock [at night] as I recall. We worked on "Looking For Someone to Love" until about midnight. For some reason most of us thought that "Looking For Someone to Love" might be the A-side, and we worked on that real hard. Then, after we got it done to what we thought was our best, we started working on "That'll Be the Day." Surprising enough, we didn't work nearly as hard on "That'll Be the Day." I recall we probably made about three or four takes of that and said that we were gonna quit, 'cause by this time it was about 2:30 or 3:00 in the morning and we all had to pile in the cars and go back to work or back to school or whatever.

NORMAN PETTY
With Buddy... he'd usually not only be good on every take, he'd do something different every take. He was the first to really do that [among Petty's artists] and that's probably the reason I felt the strongest with what he was trying to do.

NIKI SULLIVAN
I was standing with the other singers, with Gary Tollett on my left, and June Clark and Romona Tollett facing me, all singing into one microphone. I was playing rhythm guitar, but it wasn't miked, so if it had been picked up at all, it would have been through our singing mike. And I don't remember how we got in the mood, but I definitely remember it being a very fun thing, laughing and cutting up.

NORMAN PETTY
On "That'll Be the Day," Jerry was actually playing pretty loose, you know, good drums. It was a very interpretive type drum, not like any R&B or country drum sound that had been done before... So I think that in "That'll Be the Day" Jerry [was] more laid back and we had everybody in at the same time. We did feel that it was going to be a demo. We weren't really trying for isolation. We were trying for as good a balance as we could get with that many people in the studio.

JERRY ALLISON
We just shucked through both songs because they were just demos and not supposed to be finished songs. We did only two takes. We did the second one just to see if we could beat the first one, then we said, "It's only a demo," so we stopped and left it at that. When Brunswick released that record as is, we just couldn't believe it.

BUDDY HOLLY (Talking with Freeman Hoover, November 2, 1957.)
Norm asked us if we'd like for him to send it in to Brunswick Records there in New York, and so we told him, "Yeah, go ahead, we can't lose, 'cause we're as far back as you could get already," so he sent it in and Bob Thiele, the A&R man for Brunswick, okayed it and put it out, and the kids all over the United States did the rest.

BOB THIELE (Coral Records executive.)
I remember [song publisher] Murray Deutch storming into my office at Coral Records, pleading with me to release a master by the Crickets, "That'll Be the Day." The master had already been turned down by Jerry Wexler at Atlantic Records, Mitch Miller at Columbia, and Joe Carlton at RCA. I listened once and said, "Let's go." I remember pleading with the Decca executives to approve a Coral release immediately, but they refused, believing that "this raucous music" would damage the image of the Coral label. After weeks of prodding, I suggested that the master be released on the reasonably inactive Brunswick label.

DICK CLARK (Host of *American Bandstand* on ABC-TV.)
Usually we didn't play a record unless it started to break somewhere else... Sometimes it was apparent that a record was breaking big in another market—we added the Crickets' "That'll Be the Day" to the play list after it took off in Cleveland.

BOB THIELE

A few weeks after it was released, we were at a convention in the Midwest somewhere. We used to check in with the New York office every day, and this one time the sales manager said, "Bob, I don't know what happened, but the distributor in Philadelphia has re-ordered sixteen thousand copies of the Buddy Holly to be shipped to him overnight.

BILLBOARD (June 10, 1957)

That'll Be the Day.....72
BRUNSWICK 55009—Fine vocal by the group on a well-made side that should get play. Tune is a medium beat rockabilly. Performance is better than material.
I'm Lookin' For Someone to Love.....72
As with the flip, the material is inferior to the rendition. The up-tempo rockabilly gets bright, vigorous treatment, and should do as well as the flip.

LARRY HOLLEY

Buddy made a good helper for me [in Larry's tile business]... We were working on a building just outside of town. Around three p.m. Buddy seemed to be real blue and I asked him what was wrong. Buddy said, "I know I can make it and I just can't get a break." He was really frustrated. He really had the blues that day, so I said, "Let's put the tools away and we'll go home and call that fellow in New York." Well, we called that fellow and he said, "Hey, Buddy, that song is going to sell a million, they're playing it on the streets right now here in New York."

PAUL McCARTNEY

"That'll Be the Day," for instance—a very exciting record. You didn't know if they were black, white, it didn't really matter. A very sort of electric sound on the radio.

"OCTOBER 1st, 1957, that'll be the day that 'THAT'LL BE THE DAY' will have sold well over a million copies." The cover of *The Cash Box*, September 21, 1957.

L to R: Bob Thiele, Joe B Mauldin, Buddy Holly (in white), Niki Sullivan, Jerry Allison and Brunswick executive Norm Wienstroer.
Photo: Colin Escott/Showtime Archives

NIKI SULLIVAN

We were at Norman's, asleep. It was early in the morning, like eight or nine a.m., and we hadn't been to bed but three or four hours because we had been working that night before. Norman came in, and he had a piece of paper in his hand. He said, "Fellows, I have some news for you, a wire from Murray Deutch," and it said something like, "'That'll Be the

Day' has reached sales of 50,000 copies, congratulations, prepare the fellows to come to New York."

BILLBOARD (July 29, 1957)
The record has been out for a while and has suddenly started to move. All the top markets report that the disc is doing well.

NIKI SULLIVAN
As I remember, [Norman] asked us who we wanted to be our manager, and either Jerry or Buddy said, "Well, Norman, why don't you be?"

GEORGE ATWOOD
Just after "That'll Be the Day" hit big, Buddy and I were driving home from Clovis about two or three a.m. and were stopped by a policeman. Luckily when he found out who we were he wanted our autographs. We both had a big laugh over that. Usually we just talked and watched the scenery while driving. At that time Joe B. [Mauldin] was just beginning to learn to play bass and Buddy used me because he wanted a strong foundation, or bottom, to his music.

JOE B. MAULDIN
I remember the first time I was asked to play with Buddy and Jerry for a dance in Carlsbad [New Mexico], I didn't know what they expected of me, so I kept it conservative. That seemed to work out well and I pretty much kept it that way.

BUDDY KNOX
Back in those days Jimmy Bowen was the worst bass player and Joe B. really wasn't that good, but he played right. He played just the old slap bass and he was more interested in playing the slap than he was in playing the right notes, but when you play a stand-up doghouse bass onstage, nobody can hear you anyway after two rows out front—so him and Jimmy never bothered to really try to play bass much, y'know.

JERRY ALLISON
Buddy and I went by [the Youth Center] one day and Joe B. was playing there with the Four Teens, and Buddy said to Joe, "Hey, do you want to play with us?" Joe said, "Well, I will as long as it doesn't interfere with the Four Teens." He started doing some jobs with us, we went to Carlsbad and all that, and we had this little joke. It seemed that with the group the Four Teens they had this deal that each member was boss for a month, and when it came time for Joe B. to be boss, he fired the other three.

JOE B. MAULDIN
I provided a cushion under Buddy and Jerry's playing. I was very basic in what I played, usually just hitting on the first and third beats—you know, half notes. I always wanted to stretch out a bit more, and I did on "Not Fade Away" and "It's Too Late," but for the most part I kept it fairly simple and clean.

GEORGE ATWOOD
Buddy and the Crickets were recording. I'd just finished a session before

theirs, and Joe B. was plunking along, he was just learning the bass at that time. So Norman invited me to record with them. He'd record the full group on one tape, then he'd go back and record Buddy, Niki and Jerry together, with a shield, a board, between them and Joe B.; and if Joe B. got it wrong, I'd go in and add a bass to it.

BOB THIELE
Murray Deutch and I were invited to Clovis, New Mexico, to receive whatever—a Western hat and a key to the city. So we flew down and that's when we met Buddy Holly. We stayed there about two or three days, and got to know everybody. I suggested we record and keep the Crickets going, but put Buddy Holly on Coral, even if it's with the Crickets. Buddy Holly on Coral and the Crickets on Brunswick. I guess I was thinking commercially. Buddy Holly was the personality, and we didn't really want to bust up the Crickets and Buddy Holly.

MURRAY DEUTCH (Executive at Peer-Southern Music Publishing.)
The first time I met Buddy and the Crickets in New York, they were real kids, straight off the farm. They were dressed in T-shirts and jeans and everything was "Mr. Deutch," not Murray. Buddy was a very quiet kid who said little until he got to know you. He kept things inside. He never talked too much but he was a very bright guy; he listened and it sunk in.

BOB THIELE
Holly seemed to me to be an extremely sensitive individual. He looked fragile—like you could blow him over. And somehow I found myself being aware of his sensitivity and trying to be careful of how I said things to him. Even with his country talk, he sounded like a gentleman. And he *was* a gentleman.

DICK JACOBS (Coral producer who supervised Buddy's New York sessions.)
I first met him when he was appearing in Brooklyn. He had silver-rimmed glasses, gold-rimmed teeth, and looked like a hick from Texas. The next time I saw him, he wore a three-button suit, horned-rimmed glasses, had had his teeth recapped, and looked like a gentleman.

JERRY ALLISON
I said to him, "If you're going to wear glasses, then really make it obvious that you're wearing your glasses." I think Phil Everly had something to do with that, too. I remember that Buddy, Phil and I went down to a place and rounded up the pair he's wearing on the *Showcase* album.

PHIL EVERLY (The younger half of the Everly Brothers.)
The whole group looked like they were hicks from the sticks. They wore the same suits they'd probably been wearing to church. And Buddy had these old-fashioned glasses. In New York City they looked like sore thumbs.

JERRY ALLISON
We had some suits we brought back from Texas which were pretty dowdy, and then we had some made in New York that were even worse than the ones we bought in Texas. So Don and Phil [Everly] told us, "You guys have got to go over to Phil's Men's Shop on Third Street."

DON EVERLY
The only publicity pictures [the Crickets] had then was one of them all down in Lubbock, Texas, in T-shirts, setting tiles on the roof.

ROY ORBISON
Back in those days I hardly ever wore my glasses onstage. I never had the nerve until Buddy started getting hot. Later on I got big black horn rims just like his.

ELLA HOLLEY
Buddy wasn't too popular. He had enough friends. But the Lubbock kids seemed to doubt he would get anywhere with his singing. It seemed to surprise them when he did.

JOE B. MAULDIN
Buddy was the most giving person to the other people around him that I've ever known. Other stars kept their musicians on salary, but Buddy said, "No, man, share and share alike. You're as much a part of this group as I am."

NIKI SULLIVAN
The one thing Norman did for us was just to let us ramble. If there was an idea there and we had it worked out in song form, then we could go into the studio and work on it until we got it the way it sounded good to everybody. Norman just let us keep going; however long it took, it didn't make any difference.

JOE B. MAULDIN
We'd rehearse at my house and Jerry's house. Seems like we rehearsed a few times over at Niki's house and a few times at Larry Holley's house, in a garage there. And then we rented a little office out on the south side of Lubbock, and set up our instruments there. And we'd go out there nearly all the time.

GEORGE ATWOOD
Buddy knew the sound he wanted. He might run down six or seven takes of a song, then he'd go back and listen to them to see what was working. He'd pick one or two he liked and then they'd go back and record some more takes.

JERRY ALLISON
Buddy's guitar playing influenced my drumming more than anything. I haven't played with anyone since that I could play with as well, because I learned to play with what Buddy played.

JOE B. MAULDIN
Buddy was very impressed by Mickey and Sylvia's "Love Is Strange." He'd listen to that song over and over, for hours. And he worked out "Words of Love" from that.

NORMAN PETTY
You see, when we did something that we thought was really stupendous in terms of production, it was always tape machine to another tape machine. It was multi-dubbing rather than multi-tracking. We would take the basic track, put it on another tape machine, go back through the control board and play it onto another tape recorder. It was real involved.

JOE B. MAULDIN
When we laid down the basic track for "Words of Love"—electric guitar, bass and drums—I thought that was it. But Buddy said, "No, wait, I've got something else I want to add to that." So Norman set it up for the overdubbing. I couldn't believe it, it sounded so great. It seems like that song just got better and better... Actually, that song was a very dangerous situation because we started losing a lot of generations by overdubbing.

JERRY ALLISON
Buddy had two guitar parts worked out that he wanted to play, before we even started to record that. I don't know just how he got the idea, but he planned to do it that way.

BOB THIELE
I remember Buddy, somewhere, thanking me for all I had done for him, which was exaggerated by him, and said he'd like to record one of my songs. Ruth Roberts, Bill Katz and I wrote "Mailman, Bring Me No More Blues" for Buddy, and he and Murray Deutch cajoled Norman Petty into recording the song in Clovis.

BILLBOARD (June 24, 1957)
Words of Love.....84
CORAL 61852—Soft, low-toned dual track vocal with bright, sharp guitar backing on a Latin-type theme. Good clear sound. Side can do business.
Mailman, Bring Me No More Blues.....80
Sock selling effort on a well-phrased, medium beat rockabilly blues. Tune has also been done by Herb Jeffries [on RCA], but attractive reading here could prove stronger version. [Coral crooner Don Cornell also cut the song.]

BUDDY HOLLY (Making a promo tape for Cleveland disc jockey Bill Randle.)
No matter which way you look at it, it's just swell of Bill Randle and the boys here at WERE in Cleveland to take so much interest in our record of "That'll Be the Day." This is Buddy Holly and the Crickets taking this special way of thanking WERE and all you folks for being so nice to us. 'Course we hope you like our record of "Words of Love," too, along with "That'll Be the Day." Yes, that'll be the day to celebrate when we have the opportunity to be with all of you folks soon. See ya later.

JERRY ALLISON
We liked Little Richard's records quite a bit, and I can assure you it wasn't easy duplicating his sound with just a

guitar and drums. So Buddy came up with this chord/lead type of playing. It was like he had to play rhythm and lead at the same time. Also, we got into playing a very syncopated kind of thing, where we'd both play the same rhythm lick, like on "Maybe Baby," that made our music sound fuller.

LITTLE RICHARD
Buddy and I were good friends. He was a nice guy and he used to idolize my music. He'd go out and do my songs before I came on. On one of our tours he invited me to his home in Lubbock, Texas, for dinner.

Little Richard and his Upsetters wail in the movie *Mr. Rock and Roll*.
Photo: Jim Dawson

JOE B. MAULDIN
I don't think Buddy was ever completely satisfied with everything we cut. If we had had 32 and 48 multitracks like they do today, I don't think we would ever have finished a song... At Petty's we basically had one mono track. If you didn't hear it on the first playback, you didn't have it, so you went back and did it all over again till you got exactly what you wanted. I really think that working in mono added a lot of spontaneity to our records. Once you got rolling, you had to let it go all the way through.

NORMAN PETTY
The voices which backed Buddy were actually not the Crickets, and what separated the Buddy Holly records from the Crickets records was the voices we dubbed on. We used two groups. The first was Billy and Johnny Pickering and Bob Lapham. They called themselves the Picks. The second group was called the Roses.

JOHN PICKERING
When Norman wanted us for the Holly sessions, he didn't need to audition us; he and Buddy knew us and had heard us perform, Norman in Clovis and Buddy in Lubbock, mostly on the radio...We didn't try to pattern ourselves after ["That'll Be the Day"]. We just filled spaces Buddy left to fill. With our experience and Norman listening, we could tell what Buddy wanted... just by listening to rhythm patterns and the empty spots he left. He gave musi-

cians and backup singers the same freedom of expression he demanded for himself.

BILL PICKERING
Oh man, when we first heard those raw versions, it was just guitar and the singing. That's about all there was to it... just Buddy and the guitar. Norman asked us to dream up a background for them. Right on the spot. We did it for "Oh, Boy!" in 30 minutes.

JOHN PICKERING
Buddy was never present at any of our "Crickets" sessions. We overdubbed his completed solo recordings while the group was touring. Norman played the tapes and we sang with them on a single microphone; one goof-up and we started all over. We did eight songs in one continuous overnight session. We had to sing them in the keys they were recorded in and that required a lot of vocal dexterity and range.

NORMAN PETTY
[Buddy] would originally be recorded dry, with no echo or anything, and later we'd dub in the voices. We'd put the original tape on one machine and go through the board and add the voices and the echo on the final tape. But never under Buddy's supervision or when Buddy was there.

JERRY ALLISON
Norman Petty had a good studio, and he was a real good engineer... He had a lot of good ideas on some of the songs, like "Peggy Sue" for instance. He deserves a lot of credit for that being a good record.

NIKI SULLIVAN
It was called "Cindy Lou," that was the original name of the song. It had a Latin beat and was titled "Cindy Lou," who I think was Buddy's niece, who inspired Buddy to write the song. During the recording session, Jerry suggested changing it to "Peggy Sue," and immediately after that Buddy said, "Well, if you'll play double paradiddles," which is a drummer's practice roll, and Jerry agreed. Within 20 minutes we had made the recording of "Peggy Sue."

PEGGY SUE GERRON
Jerry and I had been dating on and off, all during high school... So Buddy told him, "If you can play double paradiddles all the way through, we'll change it to 'Peggy Sue.'"

JERRY ALLISON
Jaye P. Morgan had a song out back then called "Dawn" that had a tympani on it. It wasn't paradiddles [a drum exercise] but it had a very similar type beat, so I threw in paradiddles to get that same kind of steady drumming sound [on "Peggy Sue"].

NIKI SULLIVAN
The problem...was that Jerry Allison was so loud on the drums that he was picking up on all the microphones. So Norman placed Jerry outside in a hallway, completely out of the studio, and we could just about

hear him out there. Jerry had to wear headphones, and of course Buddy wore headphones.

NORMAN PETTY
[Jerry] came up with this beat and we sent him into this small room by himself. Buddy and Joe B. were in the main studio and I was potting the echo signal up and down in time with the beat. Everyone thought it was a mechanical contrivance but it was just a matter of loading the [echo] chamber in time with Jerry's beat.

CHARLIE FEATHERS
Drums don't really work with rockabilly. They collide with the bass. It ain't really rockabilly if you use drums. That just turns into rock. Drums are okay on rockabilly [only] if it's a rolling lick, like Buddy Holly's "Peggy Sue"—it's rockabilly when you keep that flow going.

JERRY ALLISON
Every other guitar player strums ["Peggy Sue"] back and forth with his pick—down-up-down-up—down-up-down-up, like that. But Holly did it with just down strokes—down-down-down-down-down-down-down-down.

NIKI SULLIVAN
Buddy was having trouble switching from the rhythm position to the lead

After band practice, 1957
Photo: Jim Dawson

position on his Strat for the lead break. It broke his timing. So finally he said to me, "Niki, you get down here on the floor and when I nod my head, you reach up and move the switch for me." My big part in "Peggy Sue" wasn't even playing!

PEGGY SUE GERRON
I have to say that I feel it's a very special gift, for me personally from Buddy. Buddy got quite a kick out of it, especially after it had become a very large hit. He'd call me Song, he'd say, "There goes Song."

TRIVIAL PURSUITS (Popular question-and-answer card game, which contains over a dozen Buddy Holly questions.)
What Buddy Holly hit did he almost call "Cindy Lou"?

NORMAN PETTY
The celeste was part of the instrumentation in the studio for [my] trio. It was used as an extra voice alongside the organ. Buddy liked the sound of it. He'd play around on it in the studio, and we both agreed that we should use it on "Everyday" because it was such a delicate song.

JERRY ALLISON
We were thinking how to record ["Everyday"]—I was patting my knees, and Buddy said, "Hey, that sounds pretty good." He played acoustic guitar, with Joe B. on bass. Norman or Vi overdubbed the celeste on it later... Never set a finger on the drums on that record, never moved.

BILLBOARD (September 30, 1957)
CORAL 61885—Peggy Sue / Everyday
Holly, one of the Crickets, makes a strong solo bid on "Peggy Sue," a rockabilly item that can cop plenty of pop and c.&w. coin. Flip, "Everyday," is another strong dual-market side with a folkish flavor. Vocal gimmicks by the artist on the medium-beat tune could make a winner.

THE CASH BOX (October 12, 1957)
It's difficult for an unknown artist to come up with one good side and break into the star category. Yet here's a newcomer with two great decks both of which could zoom up the charts. The lad's name is Buddy Holly and the two sides with all the potential are "Peggy Sue" and "Everyday." "Peggy Sue" is a fast moving rock-a-billy item that could be a tremendous teenage favorite. It's got the lyrics and melody the kids want in addition to a sensational galloping-tempo guitar and drum backdrop that makes your feet jump. Holly's vocaling is terrific. "Everyday" is a more subdued side. It's a pretty romantic ballad with a lovely melody and some more outstanding instrumental gimmicks the kids will love. Hot two-sider that could establish Buddy Holly as a name to be reckoned with.

JERRY ALLISON
[Buddy] really liked "Everyday." And "Peggy Sue"—we were all pretty flipped out about that one. We said, "Man, that's weird. That's different. It sounds good."

RUSTY YORK (Cincinnati-based rockabilly singer-guitarist, best known for "Sugaree.")
I was home one day and I got a phone call from Lou Epstein, who ran the Jimmy Skinner Music Center... He called me and said, "Do you know anyone who can sing like Buddy Holly?" I said that I did, and he asked who. I said, "Me." I was just kidding. He told me that King Records wanted somebody to sing a song called "Peggy Sue" as a cover [record]. I said I'd see what I could do, went out and bought the record immediately, and learned it. He told me that they wanted me to sound exactly like Holly if I could. I went for the audition... They would put Buddy Holly's record on one turntable and play it and we'd try to play exactly like it. We finally got it close enough and [company owner] Syd Nathan said, "That's a take." I think they had it out in about two days. It did sell well in the places that you couldn't buy Buddy Holly's record.

BOB THIELE (In a December 23, 1957, telegram to Norman Petty.) Congratulations, "Peggy Sue" hit a million today.

TOMMY ALLSUP
[Buddy] knew that it would help the

L to R: Norman Petty, Bob Thiele and Buddy in Clovis with gold disc for "Peggy Sue," 1957
Photo: Showtime Archives

Norman Petty's recording studio, 1955
Photo: Jim Dawson

popularity of his songs if local bands played them at high school dances and the like, and so he rarely did anything that any ol' band couldn't play.

NIKI SULLIVAN
We would all contribute, but it was Buddy who was the basic creator.

BUDDY HOLLY (Talking with a Florida disc jockey in 1958.)
We just play it ourselves; it's all out of our heads. Usually someone performs a lead sheet and takes the arrangements from there after the record is already out.

JERRY ALLISON
We were on the road constantly, and we didn't know who wrote [the songs] until the records came out and we looked on the label. Norman changed a couple of chords in "Peggy Sue," but Buddy wrote most of it and he and I finished it. Then when it came out, Norman's name and my name were on it, but not Buddy's. I didn't like the idea at the time, not because of the money part but more of the credit part. Buddy didn't like it either.

NORMAN PETTY
I would often write the bridge because Buddy didn't like to write bridges. I wrote the bridge and the lyrics for it on "True Love Ways." It was a cooperative thing where Buddy would come up with part of the words or part of the melody.

JERRY ALLISON
We wrote "Take Your Time" in the back of the studio at Clovis, and it's not one of my favorites and my name isn't on it. Norman Petty was writing with us and the line "heartstrings will sing like a string of twine" is far too silly. Another time I had a ballad called "Think It Over" and Buddy said it was a terrible song. We changed it around and it worked as rock 'n' roll. Buddy and I also wrote "Not Fade Away" and again my name isn't on it. That verse about my love being bigger than a Cadillac is my verse. The rhythm came from "Hambone" [by Red Saunders and the Hambone Kids] and we'd heard that long before "Bo Diddley."

NIKI SULLIVAN
One day I was sitting on this sofa in Norman's studio playing this simple little riff over and over. Buddy heard it and came over to me and said, "Tell me how you do that, tell me how." I showed him and we started singing "Tell me how, tell me how," and that's how the song "Tell Me How" came about.

JOE B. MAULDIN
We all contributed ideas to the arrangements. I can't say one specific person did the arrangements, but I guess Buddy and Jerry would receive more credit than I would. I didn't contribute all that much, but I did throw in a few ideas that stuck sometimes. Norman would come up with ideas when we went to Clovis; and even on some of the songs that we

had [already] written, Norman would come up with lyric changes or chord changes—you know, musical changes. But I felt like it was minor. I didn't feel like it warranted equal writer's credits.

NIKI SULLIVAN
I really don't mean to put Norman down, but I honestly do not remember Norman making any serious changes that even stick out in my mind. I cannot remember any songs that Norman definitely had a hand in. Norman did contribute by altering what we had said—you know, the grammar, he might have changed a "but" to an "or," or what have you. And he did write out the sheet music on the songs, but that's not co-authoring. There were times when Norman felt he should have a share of the songs, and I think all of us readily agreed. We weren't going to argue. It wasn't important then, because we didn't even have a hit record at that point.

JOE B. MAULDIN
I don't think money was that big an interest to [Buddy]. If it had been, things wouldn't have gotten as screwed up as they did. We didn't have a lawyer—we just did everything on trust in each other.

LARRY HOLLEY
One night we were all working over at Mother and Dad's installing a tile floor for them. After we got it fin-

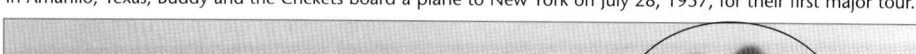

In Amarillo, Texas, Buddy and the Crickets board a plane to New York on July 28, 1957, for their first major tour.

Photo: Bill Griggs Collection

ished, Buddy and some of his friends got out their instruments and had a jam session. That was the first time I heard Buddy do "It's Too Late," a Chuck Willis number. I thought it was the prettiest song I ever heard and asked Buddy to make me a record of it the next time he was in Clovis. Well, he did, and it turned out so well that they put it on an album... It's still my favorite song by Buddy.

NORMAN PETTY (Writing instructions for the Crickets' first tour, in August of 1957, that covered several East Coast black venues with Clyde McPhatter, the Cadillacs and other R&B acts.)
Be at the Amarillo Air Terminal Sunday evening July 28th at least by 6:30 to check reservations and check baggage. Take enough cash along to pay for excess weight and meals between flights. Take about thirty or forty dollars each... the rest in Travelers Checks. Be sure to take all available identification for each member of the group.

Sign only engagement contracts and nothing more. Take extra sets of guitar strings, drum sticks, heads, etc. Take out floater insurance for entire group with everyone's name on the contract. Be sure to pack records with clothes to take on trip. Take all available clean underwear... and other articles for use on trip.

When you get to New York... take a cab directly to the Edison Hotel and check in there. We will see you about noon of that day.

Get at least two dozen Dramamine tablets... and take one tablet at least fifteen minutes before departure. Make out trip insurance to your parents. Take at least twenty-five feet of extension cord. Take small shine kit for trip. Toilet articles of your choice. Get telephone credit card and carry with you. Take a small Bible with you and READ IT! Get Hotel Credit Cards or at least make application for them. Be sure to get and keep receipts for all money spent. Be sure to send money back to Clovis for bank account.

JERRY ALLISON
The first tour we played when we left Texas was like seventeen weeks long, and I think that during that time we only had a week off, not all at one time. We went all over the U.S. and most of Canada.

NIKI SULLIVAN
We were introduced to the head of Coral Records, Bob Thiele, and he invited us to his home in upstate New York, a beautiful place with two-inch-thick carpeting. There were about six to ten people at the party, including Steve Lawrence, but mostly Coral-Brunswick [personnel]. Met Teresa Brewer, who was pregnant, a dainty, cute, wonderful, polite, sincere person—a doll; we all fell in love with her. We were asked to perform and did a four-piece vocal on an old song. Norman Petty had given us this barbershop quartet song, something like "O Baby Mine," just to prove that we were a group and could sing

together. We did it without any instruments.

JERRY ALLISON
There were a lot of songs we just didn't do on stage that much. We never played things like "Tell Me How," "I'm Looking For Someone to Love" or "Not Fade Away." The shows in those days weren't that long and you just didn't have time to play all those.

NIKI SULLIVAN
When we opened at the Howard [in Washington, D.C.], we were very well received and we were ecstatic about it, we all were. From there we went to Baltimore to the Royal Theater and we were received very well in Baltimore. There were crowds there that were a little bit unruly. There was a group called the Hearts, four young ladies that appeared on the show, and on one particular day, about the third or fourth day, somebody was drinking too much and from the balcony came a glass bottle. It hit the stage and shattered the glass and it cut one of the girls. That was the only incident that kinda marred the concert... From Baltimore we went to the Apollo Theater in New York.

TED SCOTT (Member of the black doo-wop group the G-Clefs.)
The billing on the marquee only said the Crickets, and there was a black vocal group with that name at the time. When they were booked into the Apollo, it was thought that they were booking that black vocal group. After the booking mistake, Buddy was allowed to go on anyway, and they were fantastic. The first show there was at 10:20 in the morning and the people there were saying, "What is this?" I think that Buddy and his group were shaken by playing in a black theater in a black territory, and they did get booed when they first appeared on-stage.

NIKI SULLIVAN
We had been told beforehand about the Apollo, and that if you can work the Apollo, you can work anywhere in the world. We really did not understand what they were trying to

Trade advertisement, 1957
Photo: Showtime Archives

tell us, but we did find out quickly enough. For the first two days that we were at the Apollo, we bombed. They didn't like us, they didn't like our music, and they couldn't care less that we were there. Those people had seen everything. They had seen all of the top name acts and everything else and they wanted to be impressed and entertained and we just weren't doing our job. So, I believe it was the third day just before we were to go on stage, as a matter of fact we had already been moved to the worst spot on the show, and Buddy said, "Let's open with 'Bo Diddley.'" We proceeded to go onstage, the curtains opened and we immediately went into "Bo Diddley." We really didn't know what we were doing, we didn't know many songs other than our own. "Bo Diddley" did the trick, the people liked us from that day on and we didn't have any more problems.

TED SCOTT
I thought that when I first heard Buddy Holly that he was just another white act and he would drop. After I met him, such as in the dressing room at the Apollo Theater, you could see that Buddy Holly didn't just wait around wanting to steal something. He'd listen to the other acts and artists.

JERRY ALLISON
I really got a kick out of it. We stayed at the Theresa Hotel [near the Apollo]. We were hanging out with people like Clyde McPhatter, people we'd been listening to for years. Everybody at the Apollo had already heard "That'll Be the Day," and I think they were amazed that white boys from Texas were playing it, because we were trying to sound black.

NIKI SULLIVAN
The Crickets had [our] first drink together at Jack Dempsey's. Cocktails—bourbon and Coke, which drew howls from the waiter and bartender. Coming out of a dry county, we had no experience in drinking anything but beer, at least legally. We were [in] over our heads in New York, totally green, but we snickered and made fun of everything around us.

NORMAN PETTY
[Buddy] was a ham. He loved to perform before people. All the boys did, especially Jerry Allison. They were all good hams. They loved for the audience to love them.

NIKI SULLIVAN
I was dancing around in a big circle, going through a bunch of gyrations, and Buddy was all over the stage, and Joe B. was bouncing that bass back and forth and laying it down, and I've never seen Jerry work harder on those damn drums.

JERRY ALLISON
It was really great—they were great audiences. And there wasn't any tension at all. I mean, it was really strange to us, coming from Texas where... there's a definite barrier down there.

LESLIE UGGAMS (Popular singer who caught Buddy and the Crickets at the Apollo.)
[Buddy] was terrific... sexy and wonderful... and that's what made it happen. It wasn't that [the crowd] didn't want any white acts... As long as they do a great show, that's all the audience cared about.

TED SCOTT
The tour was very strict and you had to perform every night. I never saw any drugs taken except for a few people smoking marijuana, and that was the older folks, those that had been in the business for a long time. As for Buddy Holly and his group, I can't even remember him using a cuss word, let alone taking drugs.

(At the end of August they joined an 80-day tour starring Fats Domino, Chuck Berry, LaVern Baker, the Drifters, Frankie Lymon and other top R&B and rock 'n' roll acts, starting off at the Brooklyn Paramount.)

NIKI SULLIVAN
The most outstanding thing to me was the camaraderie—everybody living and working together. Color just didn't come up. The Drifters treated me as kind of a white sheep of the family.

JERRY ALLISON
We did a lot of Little Richard's stuff like "Rip It Up," "Ready Teddy," "The Girl Can't Help It." I think we were in Wichita Falls, Texas, maybe, when we heard "Keep A Knockin'" for the first time on the radio. Buddy just said, "Hey, let's play that tonight." We played it that night at the show.

NIKI SULLIVAN
I think the real Buddy Holly was there behind the mike. Away from the mike, he was quiet, reserved, businesslike, shy—introverted, if you will. Behind the microphone, he was just like a bolt of lightning.

JERRY ALLISON
It was really a draggy old tour. I think we missed about four states. We'd get on the bus and ride and get off and pick, then get back on and ride. We all got along great. We only got to play our hits because on a lot of those shows there were 22 acts. Most of the other artists used a backup band, which gave us a better shot, because we played our own background and sounded more like our records than most of the others did.

GEORGE HAMILTON IV (Country rocker known for his 1956 hit, "A Rose and a Baby Ruth.")
Buddy Holly was the only one who had his own group—most of us worked with the pit band. It was usually an orchestra of black guys in satin suits and shirts and ties and they were more of a blues orchestra. "A Rose and a Baby Ruth" sounded very strange with brass instruments, and Buddy Holly very wisely had the Crickets with him. We would travel on buses and they weren't luxury touring buses. They were just coaches

Buddy (in 1958, right) and the Crickets (with a disc jockey in 1957, below) posed for fan photos before getting back on their tour buses

Photo: (below) Jimmie Willis

Photo: (above) Showtime Archives

with seats, no bunks in them. It was a different world then.

JERRY ALLISON
All the acts rode on two buses and slept on the seats. We got to know each other real good. Frankie Lymon was really fun to be with on the road. He was still just a kid and slept up in the luggage racks, above the seat. Paul Anka, Fats Domino and I became good buddies. We let Paul drive Fats's Cadillac. I woke up one time in the middle of the night with him practicing stopping and starting the car. We did have problems down South. We weren't allowed to stay at the black hotels. We'd have to stand around and wait for an hour, get a taxi and take it to the other part of town. That was a drag. It was against the law for a white act and a black act to appear on-stage together. One theater had a curtain down the middle of the hall—blacks on one side and whites on the other. It seems like centuries ago, but it happened in 1957.

JOHNNY MOORE (Lead singer of the Drifters.)
We went to Lubbock, Texas, and Paul Anka being the practical joker he is, hid Buddy Holly's guitar just before they called out "Buddy Holly" from the stage. Someone gave him a guitar to do his act, and when he came off, he was in a rage, he was fit to kill Paul.

The Everly Brothers joke around with Los Angeles disc jockey Art Laboe.
Photo: Jim Dawson

NIKI SULLIVAN
We were on stage in St. Louis and Paul was horsing around backstage when he kicked the microphone plug out of the floor and all the mikes went dead. We just stood there on stage, helpless. It was just a few minutes but it seemed like three or four days until the microphones got plugged back in and we could start over. At this point, Buddy was boiling up inside, just ready to explode. When we walked off, the clapping stopped the minute we got off stage into the curtains—it wasn't a very long clap. So it's totally quiet and the emcee is walking out onto the stage to introduce the next act, and Buddy yells, "Who in the hell kicked out the goddamn plug?" It rang throughout the auditorium. He calmed down after a bit and went back to the room, and later Paul Anka came back and apologized. And in fact, from that incident, Buddy and Paul became very close and even rehearsed a few songs together.

PHIL EVERLY
Buddy Holly was an exception—he would go over more on those evenings when there was a bigger male audience.

JERRY ALLISON
Holly didn't really appeal to girls as far as a teen idol sort of thing. It wasn't that they didn't dig him. They used to scream just like they did for anybody else. But... if we were out in the back loading equipment, the fans would come around and get our autographs and then if the Everly Brothers came out, they'd throw it down and hunt for a bigger piece to get the Everly Brothers' autographs. Compared to Frankie Avalon and all those slick dudes, we were just a bunch of ugly pickers who just picked.

DAVE BARTHOLOMEW (Bandleader and arranger for Fats Domino, the tour's headliner.)
I couldn't say too much about Buddy Holly. I saw him performing, he was electrifying. I thought he was electrifying, but everyone on that show had to be somebody because [they were] the stars of that year.

JERRY ALLISON
On that tour, Little Richard was the closing act, and we really got into his straight-eight kind of rhythm. Dale Hawkins was hangin' out at the shows, and he heard us do "Maybe Baby" with a swing beat. So one time he said, "Hey, why don't you do it with the same beat as 'Lucille,'" which was one of Little Richard's big hits on the show. When we got down to Tinker [Air Force Base], where Norman Petty was playing with his trio, we decided to [record] the song with a straight-eight rhythm. If you listen to the intro on "Maybe Baby," it's got the same kind of lick as 'Lucille.' We also did "Rock Me My Baby" at Tinker and it's very similar to that whole Little Richard kind of rhythm.

NORMAN PETTY
[The Norman Petty Trio] were playing in the officers club at Tinker Air Force

Poster for "The Biggest Show of Stars for '57"   Photo: Big Nickel Archives

base in Oklahoma. Buddy and the boys had some days off from a Houston gig, so they came up. I had brought my recording equipment with me and we set it up after the club closed and recorded the basic tracks to "Maybe Baby" and "Oh, Boy!" [sic], took the tracks back to Clovis and added the echo and the voices.

BUDDY HOLLY (Talking with disc jockey Red Robinson in Vancouver, Canada, October 23, 1957.)
I like "Oh, Boy!" better than "That'll Be the Day," but of course, I'm no judge.

DON EVERLY
[Buddy] and I were both Bo Diddley fans, and I'm sure he offered me "Not Fade Away." Buddy was very free with his material. I was a little more guarded. If I had something new, I'd hang onto it and save it for Phil and I, but Buddy would write something and say, "Go ahead, record it."

BILLBOARD (November 4, 1957)
BRUNSWICK 55055....Oh, Boy!
The group has a good bet to follow up their hit, "That'll Be the Day," with their strong presentation of this frantic rockabilly. Wild sounds and hollering build a lot of excitement. Flip is an interesting interpretation of an off-beat piece of material called "Not Fade Away."

CASH BOX (November 1957)
Disk of the Week... It's rare when a follow-up record is better than the artist's original hit. But that's the case

Trade advertisement, 1957
Photo: Showtime Archives

with the new Crickets release "Oh Boy." It's an exciting rock and roll sequel to the boys' tremendous smash "That'll Be the Day," a tune that's still riding high on all charts. It's a thrilling up-beat swinger that should win many new teenage fans into the Crickets' fold. The side has everything the kids want in R&R music and should bounce up onto the charts in short order. The companion piece "Not Fade Away" is another exciting teen item that should capture the attention of the kids. It's a rockin' Bo Diddleyish jumper with guitar and tom toms supplying only the backdrop. And a pause-rhythm gimmick makes the side exciting. Fine coupling the kids will flip over.

JERRY ALLISON
If we were on the road and Buddy needed strings, we'd usually pop into a drugstore and buy Black Diamonds, flat-wound or acoustic, that's all the choice there was. I remember one time we were on tour with Eddie Cochran who played a big Chet Atkins model Gretsch... Eddie would be in the dressing room for hours trying to tune it, and Buddy would come along and take his Strat out of the case and it would be in perfect tune; he'd just plug in and start picking.

JOE B. MAULDIN
Most of the stuff we did was just guitar, string bass and drums, and if that guitar wasn't singing, you'd lose it. So Buddy worked hard at keeping that guitar saying something all the time—keeping it really busy—using open strings and full chords. He'd rarely go to single string things, because there would be a gaping hole in the sound if he did.

WAYLON JENNINGS
I think [Buddy] was a rhythm player. That doesn't take anything away from his lead playing, but basically the thing that turned him on was rhythm, and that's where he was at. You know, "Peggy Sue," the biggest hit he had—the break in it was even rhythm.

JERRY ALLISON
I can't speak for everybody, but I was pretty nervous all the time. Because it all happened so fast and it seemed like we went straight from setting tile to being on network TV shows. But I was definitely more nervous on TV than I was on regular shows, and I think Buddy was too. After all, we had picked plenty—we knew we could play it and all that. And in front of people that wasn't a hang-up. But as far as TV, that was something different—an audience that wasn't there. And also, on the second Ed Sullivan show, they had fixed up a big riser for the drums—it was maybe ten feet tall. So I was sitting way up there and Joe B. was standing on one side of the riser and Niki on the other, and Buddy was out front singing. And of course the amps just went right out front and out the back and I couldn't hear a thing. And when we did the first rehearsal, Buddy said, "I can't hear the drums good—just take that thing down."

BUDDY HOLLY (Talking to Ed Sullivan on national TV, December 1, 1957)
Well, we've had a few rough times, I guess you'd say, but we've been real lucky gettin' it this quick.

JERRY ALLISON
That was the high point for me—the New York Paramount show [Christmas, 1957]. There were all kinds of people on the show, like maybe twenty acts, and we did better than anyone else as far as getting encores and all that—like nobody else would get an encore and maybe we'd get two or three sometimes.

JOE B. MAULDIN
Buddy was always one for saying, "The hell with the billing, man, I

New York Paramount marquee, Christmas, 1957
Photo: Jim Dawson

The Crickets perform live on *The Ed Sullivan Show*, December 1, 1957
Photo: Jim Dawson

want the money." When we played the New York Paramount on the Alan Freed Christmas show, Fats Domino and Jerry Lee Lewis were both billed above us, but I know for sure that we were making more than Jerry Lee and I think we were making more than Fats.

JIMMIE RODGERS (Folk-style rock 'n' roller whose "Honeycomb" was a number-one 1957 hit.)
I worked with Buddy at the old Paramount Theater in New York. Buddy was a real interesting guy. We were doing five shows a day, we'd go

out and do one at one o'clock and they'd have a movie and we'd do one at three o'clock and then a movie, another at six, another movie... Buddy was very quiet, his band used to fight, oh man, they used to fight. Those guys were tough, just kids having a good time... Most of the shows we were doing were far out, for those days. The kids would scream from the time you walked out on-stage till the time you would leave, they'd never really hear any of the lyrics or anything. You just moved your head and nine thousand kids would scream, you couldn't do any of the ballads or anything like that. I think Buddy was like me in a sense, very shy and quiet and it was kind of a big surprise to him. I've got a pair of Buddy's shoes somewhere at home, he left them in the dressing room and I took them home.

NIKI SULLIVAN
We got back [from the tour], and I was very tired; we all were. We were over at Clovis, and I just said, "Buddy, I want to quit, I'm just not happy." Buddy didn't understand why, but he didn't pursue it. He just said, "Well, Niki, if that's what you want to do." So we had a meeting of everyone in Norman's office and I said, "Fellas, I enjoyed it and everything, but that's it," and I walked out and went home. At no time did I ever hold any animosity towards Joe B., Jerry or Buddy. But my leaving the group could have been resolved, I think, with a night's sleep—just some rest.

NORMAN PETTY
The biggest rub was between Jerry and Niki. And Buddy went along with Jerry... What was there to patch up? I knew that Jerry and Joe B. and Buddy wanted him to leave, and on the other hand that Niki wanted to leave.

NIKI SULLIVAN
You put four young kids from Texas— we all were into a lifestyle where you live together 24 hours a day, and you're awake most of the time— you'll have some moments there where you'd want to be doing something else. It's a lifestyle that I was not comfortable with. That, along with the fact that we were having money problems and so forth, was the reason I quit.

JERRY ALLISON
Niki Sullivan left the group after that first tour. He wanted to go out on his own and be a singer, and had gotten a contract with Dot Records. He wanted to be on his own, and I got the feeling that he didn't think he was adding much to the band, since Buddy played all the lead guitar.

JOE B. MAULDIN
After about three months on the road, Niki on a few occasions mentioned to me that this kind of life was not for him and that he was going to try to get out and make a record deal on his own. And my response was, "Hey man, do whatever you think you need to do." When Buddy and Jerry and I would discuss

it, they'd say, "If he wants out, all he has to do is walk."

NORMAN PETTY
All the keyboards were played by either me or Vi, my wife. For example, Vi played the piano part on "Think It Over." I did the organ part on "Take Your Time" and "Valley of Tears," and maybe some other things.

JERRY ALLISON
Buddy didn't like organ at all, on anything. I never heard him say he liked it and I always heard him say he didn't like it. Sometimes he'd argue about it; sometimes he'd just save the hassle and let it ride.

NORMAN PETTY
Buddy was set in his ways as far as having some of his own ideas, and we would argue about ideas sometimes. I think that there was one thing that Buddy didn't particularly agree with me on—we used Hammond organ on "Take Your Time," sort of against his better judgment, because he felt that organ was to be reserved for church or something or other at the time, but he conceded in the end.

JERRY ALLISON
We tried to get different sounds from the regular kit—we didn't have congas or any exotic percussion instruments. I had a basic set of Premier drums, one mounted tom-tom, a snare drum and a bass drum, one crash cymbal and one rise cymbal. I played the snare drum for the tom-tom sound on "Peggy Sue," but a cardboard box sounded good on "Not Fade Away," "You're So Square" and a couple of other things.

BILLBOARD (January 6, 1958)
You Are My One Desire.....73
DECCA 30543—An interesting stylized vocal by Holly, with a triplet-marked arrangement. Performance has an intense quality.
Love Me.......72
Country blues. Holly's performance is in the authentic groove, with a country-styled string backing. As with flip, side was cut some time ago.

BILLBOARD (February 3, 1958)
CORAL 61947.......I'm Gonna Love You Too / Listen to Me
Two top efforts by Holly who's still scoring with "Peggy Sue." "I'm Gonna" is a rockabilly item with a folkish feel, and the artist renders it strongly. Flip, "Listen to Me," is also in a rockabilly groove and figures to be in there too. Tri-market appeal.
BRUNSWICK 55053......Maybe Baby / Tell Me How
Two likely successors to the group's previous clicks. "Maybe Baby" is rockabilly, and the crew gives it their usual exuberant delivery. "Tell Me How" is a rock-a-calypso type that is belted with the same appeal. A threat in all markets!

SONG HITS MAGAZINE (February 1958)
Not too long ago, the Brunswick label, hit-wise, was a pretty quiet one. Yet in the space of 24 short hours,

Trade advertisements, 1958
Photos: Showtime Archives

their name became a word on everybody's lips, as their fantastic foursome, the Crickets by name, had a big one on their hands. "That'll Be the Day" was the tune that had everybody bouncing along the streets of Main St., U.S.A., and in an effort to keep the Brunswick turntables spinning, the gang has just come out with their latest bombshell, a blockbustin' affair entitled "Oh, Boy!" And "Oh, Boy" are the magic words these days for the Crickets.

Commonly a nighttime visitor, the cricket is a music maker whose chirping sounds make the rounds "in the evening by the moonlight." Yet, night or day, no matter where you are, you can't escape the melody of musicland's Crickets, a roundup of youngsters who have already left their mark in 1957's parade of newcomers who have hit big. "That'll Be the Day" caught on so quickly, that before the Brunswick folks knew it, the phones were ringing, and the mail was cascading in, requesting the services of their brand new artists; for, like the storybook land that it is, the wonderful world of music not only readily accepted the Crickets, but gave them a million platter seller—on their first record! The "Ayes" of Texas, three of the four Crickets hail from the Lone Star State. Buddy Holly (who currently is riding high on Coral with his "Peggy Sue") is the senior member of the group. The bespectacled 21 year-older is the lead singer of the outfit, playing the guitar as well. Hailing from Lubbock, Texas, Buddy is joined by a fellow townsman in the person of Joe Mauldin on bass. Nineteen years have elapsed since Jerry Allison first began wailing his way in Hillsboro, Texas (August 31, 1938), while the "foreigner" to the Crickets, Nick [sic] Sullivan, glides in with his West-coast guitar rhythms via the reaches of South Gate, California.

BUDDY HOLLY (Talking to disc jockey Red Robinson in Vancouver, 1957.)
I think [rock 'n' roll's] going out quite a bit in the States... It might pick back up, but I rather doubt it... I'd hop on the trend [if music changed] because I'd prefer singing something a little more quieter anyhow.

JERRY ALLISON
I remember the airplane that took us [to Australia]. It had a bunch of little compartments for the passengers... It was a weird airplane, and it even had sleepers for the first-class folks. Jerry Lee Lewis and Paul Anka were on that tour with us, and they were pillow fighting on the airplane, and finally, [the staff] moved everyone else out of our compartment and turned us loose and said, "Okay, you can do your thing."

BUDDY HOLLY (Talking with Australian deejay Pat Barton in Newcastle on January 31, 1958.)
Well, I don't think [Elvis's being drafted into the Army] alters anything real outstanding in the music business. Presley will probably be a little unpopular for a while, but I think he'll come back into it, into his own after he gets out.

JERRY ALLISON
We met Johnny O'Keefe who was like the Elvis Presley of Australia. He did "Real Wild Child," which I thought was very funny. When I did it [for Coral Records, under the name Ivan], I was trying to sing like Jimmy Cagney and Buddy was playing the guitar licks. I think it sold 27 copies.

NORMAN PETTY
It was always a contest between Buddy and Jerry Lee to see who could get the wildest reaction. It was a game between them.

Jerry "Ivan" Allison, Coral Records publicity shot
Photo: Jim Dawson

JERRY LEE LEWIS
In Australia he got four encores and nearly took the show away from me... Buddy was the real star on that one. He just tore them up over there—just drove them wild.

STAN ROFE (Popular Melbourne, Australia, disc jockey.)
I first met Buddy Holly at the old Chevron Hotel in St. Kilda. The Chevron, in the early days, was where all the rock 'n' roll stars stayed, at least that's where [promoter] Lee Gordon put them, either at the Chevron or at the Savoy Plaza at the other end of town... I had to wait for Buddy in the foyer. I had already made a phone call to ask him if he would have a talk with me, and he said he would have morning coffee. What I hadn't realized was that I was waiting at the Chevron to see Buddy Holly when in actual fact I had not

During a Florida tour in the spring of 1958, Buddy shows Jerry Lee Lewis a note, while Jimmy Velvet and Phil Everly look on.

Photo: Showtime Archives

recognized the man. He was sitting about 50 yards away from me having coffee anyway and it was about half an hour before I had realized it was Buddy Holly sitting there alone having coffee in the little lounge room.

FRANK IFIELD (British-born Australian singing star, best known for "I Remember You.")
I was very fortunate to be on the bill when he played the Sydney Stadium in 1958. The whole guy was such an anti-image. Most rock 'n' roll artists were trying to be flamboyant sex symbols, but he was like a college kid, thin and bespectacled, and wearing your glasses onstage was unheard of in those days. He looked like he lacked confidence, but the magic was in his sound. He showed that you didn't have to be glamorous to be noticed. He also was a very nice man to talk to.

STAN ROFE
I suppose you couldn't call Buddy Holly electrifying because he really didn't move a lot onstage, although he was into a few of the [moves]... I think Buddy relied on his music more than anything else to get him over. His music, perhaps, was more electrifying than his presence, but then again, because the music was so damn good you couldn't help but admire the man.

BUDDY HOLLY (Talking to Alan Freed in New York City, September 23, 1958.)
I was just into town the other day in Cincinnati, remember when we landed there? And the helicopter had crashed that day that we got in there.

ALAN FREED
We toured together for forty-four days. He was a bug for flying.

Alan Freed
Photo: Allen Day

(**After returning from Australia, Buddy, Joe B., Jerry and Norman and Vi Petty flew into London on February 28, 1958, to begin a month of touring throughout the U.K.**)

LARRY PAGE (British singer, dubbed "The Teenage Rage.")
I was signed by EMI, and as I was working for them as a record packer, I was packing my own records. They found a song that I was told would never be released in this country called "That'll Be the Day." I recorded it with the Geoff Love Orchestra and the Rita Williams Singers, but it was a silly arrangement with no feel, and the minute we hit the market, the Crickets' record was released [in the U.K.], which went straight to number one. If you buy the original music sheet, you'll find my face on it and not Buddy Holly's. The only good thing about the whole episode is that I got a chance to meet Buddy Holly when he came to England. He was in full white cricket gear because they were doing a promotion on the Crickets.

JOE B. MAULDIN
When Buddy and I and J.I. came over to England in 1958, we were the rock 'n' roll act on a variety show. There was Des O'Connor, Gary Miller, the Tanner Sisters and the Ronnie Keene Orchestra. I thought that was the

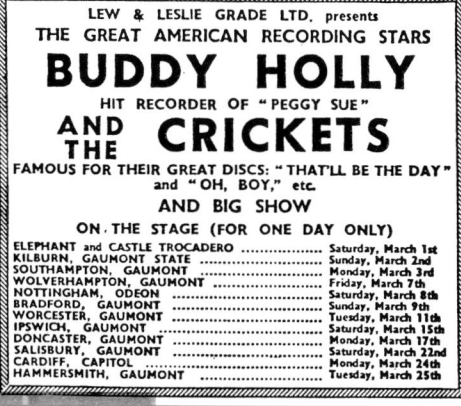

(top) Trade advertisement of British tour performances

(left) Buddy and the Crickets in the U.K. appearing on the BBC show *Off the Record* in March, 1958. L to R: Joe B., Buddy and Jerry.

Photos: Showtime Archives

Buddy and the Crickets perform at the Windsor Arena, Ontario, April 9, 1958
Photo: Jim Dawson

Photo: Showtime Archives

Buddy rocks London, March 1, 1958
Photo: Showtime Archives

deal over here, that people wanted to see a variety show rather than straight rock 'n' roll. In America we had done the Alan Freed shows with 21 different acts, who were all rock 'n' rollers. They'd say, "And now the Crickets," and we'd do two tunes, then it was, "And now Eddie Cochran," and he only got one song. It was quite different here 'cause we got to play for thirty minutes.

BUDDY HOLLY (Talking with reporter Keith Goodwin of *New*

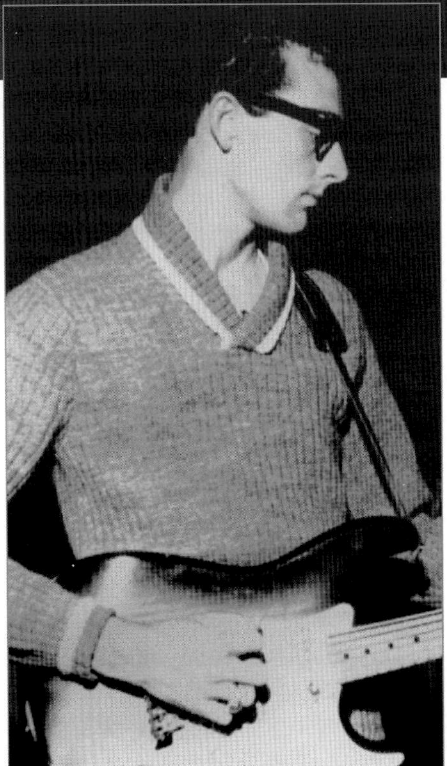

(top) Fooling around during rehearsals at the Trocadero Theater, Elephant and Castle, London, March 1, 1958
Photo: Showtime Archives

Buddy backstage at the Trocadero
Photos: Showtime Archives and John Beecher

Musical Express.)
You know what happened there [at the State Kilburn Theater]? I broke a string for the first time. It kind of put us off balance for a while, but everything went along fine when I got it repaired.

DES O'CONNOR (All-round British entertainer and comedian.)
I got 100 pounds a week for being the [emcee] and comic on Buddy Holly's tour, which was big money then. We were touring with the Ronnie Keene Orchestra, which had 28 musicians with a front line of 16 brass, and then out come the Crickets, just three of them, and I couldn't make out how they were making ten times as much noise. It was so exciting and vibrant and I knew that something exciting was happening.

LONNIE DONEGAN (One of Britain's most popular recording acts in the latter 1950s, who sparked the skiffle movement and recorded such international hits as "Rock Island Line.")
I met Buddy Holly and the Crickets over a cup of tea when they played in Britain. He was the first person to bring a solid guitar into the country, and because of the rulings with the Musicians Union, it was very rare to see an American singer with his own band. I'd never seen a drummer like Jerry Allison before. He was all over his kit. It was great Texas drumming.

BUDDY HOLLY (Talking to *Melody Maker* magazine.)
We've been going a year and one always wonders how long it's going to last. But so far the public seems to like us and we hope that as long as we don't make any mistakes, we'll be all right.

MICK JAGGER (To his friend, drummer Dick Taylor, after seeing the Crickets at the Woolwich Granada, March 14, 1958—the first rock 'n' roll show he'd ever attended.)
That was a gas!

DICK TAYLOR (Drummer with Mick Jagger's earliest band.)
[Jagger] was absolutely transfixed—you could see the wheels going round in his head, trying to learn as much as he could. It was great, terrific—the first time we heard the Buddy Holly classic "Not Fade Away."

KEITH RICHARDS (Guitarist of the Rolling Stones.)
Mick had been singin' with some rock and roll bands, doin' Buddy Holly... Buddy Holly was in England as solid as Elvis. Everything that came out was a record smash number one. By about '58, it was either Elvis or Buddy. It was split into two camps. The Elvis fans were the heavy leather boys and the Buddy Holly ones all somehow looked like Buddy Holly.

PAUL McCARTNEY
Buddy came along and he was a fellow with glasses, and you'd never really seen anyone with glasses. It always seemed that anyone who had glasses couldn't make it as a singer, so at least they'd have to take their glasses off and have contacts in or

something. But suddenly this singer appeared, you know, these big horn-rimmed specs, and we were getting ready to start the Beatles and thinking of making a group. So John—John Lennon—who normally wore the horn-rimmed specs but always took them off onstage, he was now able to put them on and see the world.

JOHN LENNON
He made it okay to wear glasses. I *was* Buddy Holly.

PAUL McCARTNEY
One thing I remember is Sunday Night at the [London] Palladium, they used to have a big variety [TV] show, and Buddy was on that once. That was the big occasion to watch his fingers, see what guitar he had, see if he played the chords right and how he did that solo on "Peggy Sue," see if he used the capo or not.

BUDDY HOLLY (Talking to Keith Goodwin of *New Musical Express*.)
The equipment you have in your theaters puts most American halls to shame. We're really impressed by the technical aspect of show business in Britain, and the smooth running of the London Palladium TV show, which we did on our second day here, was something to be marveled at.

JOHN LENNON
I only saw [the Crickets] on the London Palladium (on TV). He was great! It was the first time I saw a Fender guitar! Being played! While the singer sang! Also, the secret of the drumming on "Peggy Sue" was revealed... live.

BUDDY HOLLY (Introducing the song "Rip It Up" onstage, as reported by the British press.)
Here's a sad little song with tender lyrics that really tell a story. This tune is likely to reduce you all to tears, not because of the sadness of the words, but on account of the pathetic way we sing it.

GERRY STANDARD (Liverpool fan.)
I still have my ticket for the second performance at the Liverpool Philharmonic—seat D24, cost four shillings. While we were waiting outside, the first house came out and some of them were offering us double price for our tickets so they could go in again. Des O'Connor's introduction, with a wave of the hand, was simply, "Ladies and gentlemen, Buddy Holly and the Crickets." The group ran onstage, Jerry to the drums, Joe to the double bass and Buddy to the center. He already had his guitar around his shoulder. They began with "Oh, Boy!" and Buddy said, "It's great to be in Liverpool, but who wants to hear me talking? Let's get on with the music." They also did "Ready Teddy," "Rip It Up," "Everyday," "Not Fade Away" and "That'll Be the Day." They took three curtain calls and then did "That'll Be the Day" again. It was a night I'll remember for the rest of my life.

BUDDY HOLLY
We like to think that we play rhythm and blues with country and western overtones, and my personal favorites

The boys tour London's Austin car plant.
Photo: Showtime Archives/Jim Carr

Crickets' Joe B. Mauldin jives with a fan at the Crickets' U.K. press reception held at the Whiskey-A-Go Go Club in Soho, London.

Photo: Showtime Archives

Buddy and the Crickets meet England's legendary cricket players, Denis Compton (at left) and Godfrey Evans.

Photo: Showtime Archives/Pictoral Press

in this field are Elvis Presley, Ray Charles, the Everly Brothers and Eddie Cochran. We also like Little Richard and do some of his numbers in our act.

MIKE PENDER (Member of the '60s British rock group the Searchers.)
I saw Buddy Holly at the Liverpool Philharmonic, and from that night onwards, everything I learned, everything I played, was based on Holly. Groups now have banks of amplifiers and speakers all over the place, and most times they still don't get the sound they want. Holly went onstage with just a double bass, drums and one amplifier. He didn't have any sex appeal and he wasn't that good looking, but he brought the house down. A lot of people have tried to imitate him over the years but nobody's ever got close.

BUDDY HOLLY (Writing a letter to his parents from Salisbury, England, March 22, 1958.)
Dear Mother and Dad, I thought I would drop one more letter to you before we leave England and I figured it had better be now or we would get to the states before the letter. We probably will anyhow but—there you are.

We had three good shows today. The last one especially. We are getting to where we can carry on pretty good on the stage what with a few little jokes and all. Everyone commented on how my jokes get bigger laughs than the comedian on the show, Des O'Connor. Who knows, we might change and be comedians instead of rock & roll stars.

I guess you are wondering by now why I am writing this way. Jerry and I bought some new pens today, and they write good this way so I thought I'd try it.

Norman and Jerry are sitting over by the fireplace (this is a real old, quaint place) talking about dreams. Norman was just telling about a dream he had where all his teeth came out. I guess he's just getting old?

I was glad to hear that you are getting something done on the house. I wonder what it will look like when it's finished. Just have to wait I guess.

Well, I guess I'll close for now and talk to you when we get to New York. Til' then, bye for now. Love, Buddy.

DES O'CONNOR
Someone published a letter that Buddy wrote home in which he said his jokes were going down better than mine, the little stinker. What he didn't say was that I was giving him the jokes. He had a real Southern drawl and I helped him to modify it so that the English would understand him. The audiences loved his accent, and jokes that I wouldn't get laughs with would be downright funny when he delivered them.

BUDDY HOLLY (Talking with *New Musical Express*.)
Back home in the States, most of our time is taken up with big package shows that tour from coast to coast... These package shows really are mammoth affairs. Sometimes there are as

many as 18 or 20 acts in the show. Some artists do only one number, but this of course depends entirely on how many records that particular artist has got moving at the time... The traveling distances in the States probably sound enormous to you. We look upon journeys ranging from 200 to 300 miles as small hops and do these either by bus or rail. Anything over 400 miles is made by air. So you see, the journeys we're making between dates in Britain are really small to us and aren't any bother at all.

BRIAN POOLE (Lead singer of Brian Poole & the Tremeloes, a popular '60s British rock group.)
Buddy Holly and the Crickets were absolutely marvelous because they were the loudest thing we'd ever heard. It was a small band, but they made such a crack when they came on and it was very, very exciting, and that's when we had someone to look up to. We developed our style and we were doing Buddy Holly songs for the next five years.

MELODY MAKER MAGAZINE (Anonymous writer.)
I went to hear them at the Trocadero, Elephant and Castle, on Saturday where, despite a Presley film across the road, they drew 1500 into the first house and 3000 to the second. And I might as well say now that, although it's an excellent show, I was disappointed that Buddy Holly & the Crickets were on stage little more than 20 minutes... Strangely enough, they unload all their disc hits with feverish speed... I didn't feel quite at home with Buddy Holly when he added the Presley movements. He seems so obviously out of his depth. But, although I did detect a few scornful laughs, it produced the usual screams from the usual bevy of teenagers.

PETER HOLDSWORTH (Reporter for the Bradford, Yorkshire, *Telegraph and Argus*.)
They were Americans Buddy Holly and the Crickets. Unless they had previously read the lyrics or heard them sung by an articulate vocalist, I would have defied anyone in the audience to tell me what seventy per cent of the words were which issued from the lips of this foot-stomping, knee-falling musician. Where on earth is show business heading?

KEITH GOODWIN
Much of the trio's success can be attributed to the fact that their "in person" sound is almost identical to the sound that they produce on record... Without doubt, the Crickets are the loudest, noisiest trio I've ever heard in my life. But how these boys manage to make such a big sound with their limited instrumentation baffles me!

JOE COCKER
I remember [Buddy] having a huge guitar lead, a long cord that stretched the length of the stage, but he didn't impress me.

JERRY ALLISON
We had a really good time [in

England]. It was cold and the beer was warm, which was strange for us. The British audiences were more reserved during the songs, but they really grooved afterwards.

JOE B. MAULDIN
All the hotels had a small heater on the wall that you had to put a sixpence in, and we were running out of sixpences. By the time we got some more, the room had gotten cold again, so we usually stayed downstairs by the fireplaces.

DES O'CONNOR
We traveled together on the bus and I shared a room with Buddy a couple of times. I was the only one who could drag him out of bed. He was a devil to wake up, and the only time he wasn't smiling was in the mornings. When we walked around Soho, he went into a music shop and tried about seventeen guitars. They all sounded the same to me, but he picked a Gibson, said it had a good tone and bought it. He'd play it on the bus and he showed me how to play guitar. He taught me C, F and G, but I wasn't meant to be a guitar player. When he left he gave it to me. He said, "You use this, Des, I've got too many of them anyway." There are in-built memories with that guitar, but as I'm still on C, F and G, I don't think he'd be too thrilled with his pupil.

JOE B. MAULDIN
We had been in England a month and it was cold and it seemed like we'd been away from home forever. I had a great big cigar and I said, "I'm gonna celebrate, man, I'm gonna smoke this cigar." Well, it was cold, and all the windows were closed in this small dressing room [at the Hammersmith Gaumont on March 25], and Jerry and Buddy said, "You're not smoking that cigar in here." So we started scuffling... But when I swung around, Buddy bent down to get the cigar, and instead of hitting him in the stomach, I hit him in the mouth with my head and knocked off two of the caps on his teeth... So what Buddy did was, he chewed some gum and then mashed the gum out and smoothed it over his teeth, and I guess from the audience you couldn't tell the difference.

ROY ORBISON
I was in a restaurant in Nashville one time with the Everly Brothers having lunch. Buddy Holly came in and said he'd just been to England, and it was magnificent.

PHIL EVERLY
Don and I didn't have a band in those days. The booking agent [in Florida] had supplied us with three high school boys, who really couldn't play. We were stuck. So Buddy Holly and the Crickets volunteered to play for us... Without Buddy and the Crickets, I really don't know if we could have followed Jerry Lee [Lewis] at the time. Only by the grace of God, and Buddy Holly and the Crickets, did Don and I manage to pull it off. It was one of the best shows we ever did.

JERRY ALLISON
I can remember when we were down in Florida one time, we [the Everly Brothers and the Crickets] were traveling in two station wagons. Well, each car had about a dozen eggs that we were throwing at the other. It sounds real crazy now... but to see these two station wagons with a bunch of guys throwing eggs at each other was very funny.

JOE B. MAULDIN
The electric [bass] gives you more control and more volume, but it also makes your mistakes stick out. Buddy didn't seem to mind that I wanted to use an electric on the road, but he definitely didn't want to use it in the studio. He was tickled over the sound we were getting with the standup, and he wanted to keep it that way.

SONNY CURTIS
"Well... All Right" is one of my favorites of Buddy's songs. His version just featured his acoustic guitar and Jerry Allison playin' on the top of his cymbal, y'know, and it just sounded so different for that time.

JERRY ALLISON
We wrote it because Little Richard used to go around saying, "Well, all right!" So we said, "Let's write a song for Little Richard."

JOE B. MAULDIN
I was fortunate enough to get in on the writing of "Well... All Right." We would all throw in a line here and there, so it is hard to say who exactly wrote what on it.

Buddy horses around with Waylon Jennings, 1959.

Photo: Jim Dawson

WAYLON JENNINGS
I'd known Buddy for about six or seven years; we'd played in contests around Lubbock and at KDAV. He was like a hero in Lubbock—still is. Nothing really happens out there; you just sit around and listen to your hair grow. I was a disc jockey, and Buddy was the first person—outside of my own family—to ever believe in me as a singer... I was his protégé more or less. He cut the first record on me, you know, for Brunswick in 1958. Got King Curtis to play on it, just called him to come down, he was really hot then, too. We did an old [Cajun] thing called "Jole Blon,"

we did it upbeat, with the saxophone on the lead part. We didn't even know the words.

NORMAN PETTY
[King Curtis] had played in New York before he got on the plane to fly to Lubbock. Buddy picked him up, brought him over and did "Reminiscing," "Come Back Baby" and a separate session with Waylon Jennings... We recorded all night, well into the early morning. King Curtis had to be back in New York to play that night, so Buddy rushed him to Lubbock to get him back to New York in time.

WAYLON JENNINGS
Buddy played guitar [on "Jole Blon"]; I didn't play a thing on that session. Basically, I was just hangin' out. King Curtis was playing saxophone, and I was just marveling a whole lot.

BILL TILGHMAN
We were driving up and down the street in my home town, Sonny [West] and I, and we grabbed onto that title ["Rave On"] and said, "Let's do something with it." First we wrote it as a domestic problem, a disagreement between two people, but Norman turned it down—he told us to bring it back, he wanted us to write a love song out of it. So we worked on it a couple of weeks, to the way it is now, and took it back over.

BOB THIELE
He always wanted to record in New York... Anyway, he did get to New York, but we wound up with only two sides. We did a thing called "Rave On" and a standard, "That's My Desire." "Rave On" was tremendous. We did that on Eighth Avenue in a hot studio at the time. I didn't want to use the Decca studio, so we used Bell Sound. At least at Bell, unlike at Decca, we could isolate musicians. It was a dead-sounding studio, the sound wasn't traveling all over the place.

JERRY ALLISON
The idea was that the Crickets' records should have overdubbed, background voices and Buddy Holly's should just feature the single voice. That lasted about six months, because we then recorded "Rave On" in New York and we had some guys come in and sing background vocals.

BILLBOARD (April 21, 1958)
CORAL 61985.......Rave On / Take Your Time
Holly appears to be back in chart form on "Rave On," a rockabilly item that he belts with hiccupy gusto. "Take Your Time" is a less frantic effort, but it also has the money sound. Also a strong bet for c.&w. coin.

DISC JOCKEY AT WRC IN WASHINGTON, D.C. (On a special radio spot sales LP called *Music to Buy Time By*, which was sent to advertising agencies across the country in late 1958.) This first little gem features one of the rocking immortals, a real talent by the name of Buddy Holly. [Record starts playing.] What'd he say? What? That was Buddy Holly with mood music for stealing hub caps. "Rave On," it's called. Humph! You know, for a few seconds there it did.

JERRY ALLISON
A lot of Buddy's songs had a certain attitude—like "That'll be the day, when you say goodbye," sort of "I don't need you." Or "Think It Over"—you know, "think it over in your pretty little head—are you sure I'm not the one?" That was his attitude about everything. Because he was really a self-confident, smart-aleck sort of guy, you know. He'd say anything he wanted to. He wasn't ever trying to be really nice to people, he'd just say what he thought.

BILLBOARD (June 2, 1958)
BRUNSWICK 55072.......Think It Over / Fool's Paradise
Good group vocals on both of these rockabilly efforts make each a strong contender in pop and c.&w. marts. "Think" is a medium-tempo tune that is helped by wild piano support. "Paradise" is a countryish theme that is also given a strong rendition against plucked string backing.

THE CASH BOX (June 28, 1958)
(Decca 30650) GIRL ON MY MIND—From his Decca LP *That'll Be the Day* comes this rock-a-billy single. Dramatic romancer chanted commercially by the popular performer. TING-A-LING—Another good rock-a-billy swinger with an exciting echo vocal by Holly. Side is also from the Holly LP.

JERRY ALLISON
Bobby Darin was on Atco, which was a division of Atlantic Records. He thought he was going to be dropped and so he cut "Early in the Morning" and "Now We're One" with the Rinky Dinks for Coral, another label entirely. Atco didn't drop him, the contract continued, and so they had to give that record back to Atco. Coral thought it was a good record, and in an emergency record deal they got Buddy to cut it in New York—and the Rinky Dinks were the backup on that too. He really thought ["Early in the Morning"] was an excellent record. He liked having the black chorus [the Helen Way Singers] on it. When I heard the record, I thought at the time, "This is the best record so far." My feelings weren't hurt by not playing on it—after all, I wasn't even in New York when he cut it.

BILLBOARD (June 30, 1958)
CORAL 62006...........Early in the Morning / Now We're One
"Early" is a swinging blues, and Holly belts it solidly against a New Orleans beat. "Now," the flip, is also a snappy blues, and the performance accorded is equally powerful. Both sides were written by Bobby Darin. Disk could click in all markets.

JERRY ALLISON
We never did any of the rock 'n' roll films because Norman Petty was waiting for the big parts. We wanted to make some, but Norman said, "No, no, we'll wait for a legit movie." I don't think he liked rock 'n' roll movies. I don't think he liked rock 'n' roll sometimes.

MARIA ELENA SANTIAGO HOLLY
One morning the Crickets came into the office [where I worked] to see Murray Deutch. He was tied up just then, so they sat in the outer office to wait. I had never met them before, at least I don't think I had seen them, and I know I had never been introduced to them. They were joking around, imitating a Spanish accent and changing English words so they'd sound Spanish, and they introduced each other to me that way. When Deutch was free, they went in to see him, and when they came out, Buddy asked me when I'd be free for lunch. Well, when you're a receptionist, you're supposed to greet people and be pleasant to them and not take everything they say too seriously. So I told him I wouldn't be free for a couple of hours. "Okay," he said, "we'll be waiting for you."

At lunch time, Jo Harper, who was in charge of NorVaJak business at Peer-Southern, asked me where I was going to eat. I told her I was just going to go downstairs, and she said, "No, come out with me—let's go over to the Howard Johnson's." "Why there?" I asked. And Jo said, "I've got to bring some papers over to Norman Petty and he's waiting for me there." So I said okay. When we went, Norman was there, all right, but that wasn't why Jo had insisted on eating there. You see, the Crickets were there too—Buddy had called Jo Harper and set the whole thing up, telling her to get me down there somehow.

BUDDY HOLLY (To his fellow musicians, at Howard Johnson's.) You see this girl? I'm going to marry her. And I'm going to get her to agree in the next two days, before we leave New York.

The Hollys (Maria Elena and Buddy) and the Allisons (Jerry and Peggy Sue) honeymoon together in Acapulco, August 1958. Photo: Jim Dawson

MARIA ELENA HOLLY
After the ["Early in the Morning"] recording session, we went out to eat at P.J. Clarke's [on Third Avenue]. And that was where he proposed to me. I didn't take him seriously at first—I thought he was joking. And he got really upset with me and said, "No, listen to me, I really mean it." And so I said yes.

BUDDY HOLLY (Talking to his mother upon his return to Lubbock.)
My girl's going to come down here and visit about a week. And then we're going to get married. Now, Mother, you might as well not say anything because I've made up my mind and I'm going to marry her.

LARRY HOLLEY
Buddy brought Maria Elena down to Lubbock in August of '58 and they were married in Mother and Dad's home by our preacher. We were all pleased with his pretty wife and they started living in New York.

MARIA ELENA HOLLY
Norman said that Buddy should not marry at that time... Norman knew that once I got involved, I would be finding out things that he didn't want me to find or Buddy to find, and that once I was in the picture, things would turn around.

PEGGY SUE GERRON
Maria Elena was not a girl. She was...older than Buddy, and had been raised in New York, which is very different than Lubbock, Texas. She was very attractive, she was very polished.

MARIA ELENA HOLLY
When we traveled on tour, I was supposed to be the Crickets' secretary. But everybody on the tour knew we were married and Buddy always introduced me to everyone as his wife. So it isn't true that our marriage was secret. We just didn't feel like broadcasting the news, not for a little while anyway.

JERRY ALLISON
All of a sudden it wasn't Joe B., Buddy and I hanging out.

MARIA ELENA HOLLY
Jerry and Joe B. felt a little bit intimidated by the fact that I was there and that Buddy didn't do very much without my being involved. I guess Jerry more so than Joe B. felt uncomfortable with the fact that I was making decisions.

BUDDY HOLLY (Speaking with Jerry Allison in late 1958.)
Why do we want to go out on the road and work all the time? What if you get killed tomorrow? Let's have some fun. Let's ride our motorcycles and just do what we want to do. We've got enough money—let's enjoy it.

LARRY WELBORN
I had been trying to get my own recording career started and I hadn't gotten anywhere, and I asked Buddy how he managed to come up with one successful record after another.

Buddy kind of grinned and shook his head and said, "It's getting tougher all the time. You have to keep coming up with something new—something they haven't heard before."

PHIL EVERLY
I think Buddy actually understood that this rock 'n' roll wasn't going to fade away, that a career would last many, many years... I think he had it somewhere in his mind that this thing would keep growing if you innovated. He was extremely aware, more aware of subtleties than I, and maybe had a little more faith in the music.

DON EVERLY
[Buddy] was thinking about progressing and moving on. We were all looking—we knew that you couldn't just follow that one same hit every time, you knew the music was moving along. We both tried strings, looked for outside songs, looked for different sounds. But no one quite knew what was going to happen.

WAYLON JENNINGS
He liked Mickey Baker, and he loved Ray Charles's stuff. You know, J.I. and I were saying the other day that we wished that Buddy were alive to hear "What'd I Say." He never got to hear it. [Actually, Buddy did hear it.] Buddy had a great idea, man. He was looking for the guy who arranged Ray Charles's things; he wanted to do Ray Charles's arrangements for guitars, or around guitars.

MARIA ELENA HOLLY
When we were in California in the fall, we managed to find out where Ray Charles lived and we went over to his house, but he was out on tour. Buddy was hoping to talk to Charles and see if he'd be willing to work with Buddy on [an album]—help with the arrangements and maybe play on it. Buddy really loved Charles's style and he wanted to meet him and talk with him about it.

BUDDY HOLLY (Talking to Alan Freed on Freed's TV *Dance Party*, October 2, 1958.)
Well, we haven't been working all summer, Alan, we've just been kinda loafin' and takin' it easy, and runnin' around some, enjoyin' what we hadn't enjoyed for the whole year previous, you know, all the work goin' on, so we're gettin' ready to start in with some new work now.

TOMMY ALLSUP
The first session I worked with him on was "It's So Easy," and he and Norman worked on the arrangement for hours. J.I. and myself finally went to sleep on some sofas in the studio, and they came and got us about 4:00 a.m. when they were ready to record. I was so tired I think I must have slept through the session. It seems like we did 900 takes on just about everything we did.

JOE B. MAULDIN
Buddy was a star and he knew it, and he didn't mind anybody else sharing the stardom with him. He loved the

way Tommy played; he thought he was a fantastic guitar player. Tommy knew a lot about music, too. And he was a very likable, enjoyable person.

NORMAN PETTY
Buddy was so impressed with Tommy that he asked him to play lead on some demos he was making for the Everly Brothers—"Wishing" and "Love's Made a Fool of You."

TOMMY ALLSUP
Buddy pretty much let me do what I wanted on those sides. He was very easy going, even though he really controlled the sessions. He knew exactly what sound he wanted. We both played Stratocasters, as that was the only real rock 'n' roll guitar at the time. I had been using Gibson strings, and I'd gotten into building my own sets [of strings] since there were no gauged sets back then. On "It's So Easy" I used an unwound second for the third, and a third string for the fourth and so on, making them lighter so I could bend notes. Buddy liked the sound we got on that number, and we did the same kind of lines on "Love's Made a Fool of You."

BILLBOARD (September 22, 1958)
Brunswick 55094..........It's So Easy / Lonesome Tears
Paced by Buddy Holly's strong vocal, the crew comes thru with a solid reading on "It's So Easy," a catchy rockabilly tune. "Lonesome Tears," the flip, is an effective change of pace on a rockaballad. Both sides are well performed, and it's a toss as to which will take over. Watch 'em!

BILLBOARD (October 27, 1958)
Heartbeat...........81
CORAL 62051—Calypso type is nicely delivered by the artist with good string backing. Tune tells of a lad whose heart skips a beat when his chick comes into view. It could happen.
Well...All Right.........80
Minor-key rockabilly is given Holly's usual fine outing. Performance matches that on flip, and potential appears similar.

THE CASH BOX (November 11, 1958)
Sleeper of the Week Buddy Holly, a veteran on the best sellers both as a single and as the lead of the Crickets, sounds as tho he has another chart item in "Heartbeat," a pretty latin tempo rock-a-ballad. Contagious melody and excellent lyric could make this a big winner. Buddy has a charming country twang in his voice here. It should win teenage approval. Flip is another good beat item.

HENRY GOLDRICH (Employee at Manny's Guitar Shop in New York.)
I knew [Buddy] well. He first came in here with Buddy Knox back in 1957. Later, he and Don Everly would come in quite a bit. I remember one time Buddy and Don came in with their wives, and they sent the girls out on a shopping spree while they stayed there for about four hours trying every guitar I had in stock.

BOB MONTGOMERY
Buddy always said he'd have himself a Cadillac by the time he was twenty-one. So he did.

JACK SCOTT (Popular Canadian rock balladeer who had several 1950s hits.) I had "My True Love" out and we were going on a tour with a bunch of people and [Buddy] was driving the car... He was at Southern Music also and he married the girl that worked at Southern Music. I met him outside the building there...just getting ready to get on the bus. He was driving his car and the rest of us were on this big bus. He was following the bus and I got to meet him at that point in time.

JOE B. MAULDIN
On that [late 1958] tour, we weren't as close as we had been before. Of course now I can understand why—Buddy was a married man and had his wife with him, and he had to devote more time to her than he did to Jerry and I. But at the time, I felt like Buddy didn't want to be a part of the group anymore, he wanted to be a bigshot star himself. And I was jealous of Maria Elena because it seemed that she was taking Buddy away from Jerry and I. Buddy had been like a brother for so long, and suddenly Buddy was no longer a brother.

BUDDY HOLLY (Talking to Dick Clark on *American Bandstand*, October 28, 1958.)
We just got off of a seventeen-day tour and, uh, I had my car on the tour and the boys had a station wagon that some of the other group went home in, and so, uh, naturally they're having to fly in [to Lubbock] because I won't let 'em ride with me.

MARIA ELENA HOLLY
I would never have stayed in Lubbock. The way they felt about blacks and Mexicans—it didn't intimidate me at all, but after growing up in New York City and being with everybody, I couldn't have stood for that sort of thinking.

JOE B. MAULDIN
There were a few conversations where Buddy mentioned, "Hey, guys, we're gonna have to move to New York, to get away from Petty." And I was somewhat confused because I didn't think that was the right thing to do. Norman had hyped us so much on the people in New York, and how we'd never see any of our money. Norman would say, "Look at all those groups that have had a bunch of hit records and they've never made a nickel—they're stone broke. They'll take it all away from you, and you'll wind up the same way."

NORMAN PETTY
[Maria Elena] told him that he didn't need the Crickets—that he didn't need me.

JERRY ALLISON
We went over to Clovis, and Norman talked us out of splitting, that's what happened. He said, "You know, you guys better hang down here. When you get to New York, you're gonna see, you'll be cheated out of everything."

JOE B. MAULDIN
I think Maria Elena, right off the bat, wanted Buddy to move to New York and get away from Norman Petty, because I think she knew what was going on with our money. She probably had access to publishing records that we didn't.

JERRY ALLISON
I really believe that if we had all stayed together in Clovis, then it would have all been squared away. We would have sat down and said, "Okay, I wrote half of that and you wrote half of this," and I think Norman would have probably said, "Right, we'll split the money that way." But when it all fell apart, then the way the contracts went—the way Norman had fixed the contracts—that was the way it stayed.

JOE B. MAULDIN
But it's not that Maria broke the group up. I felt like Petty's the one who broke the group up. Norman said, "Look, let's stay down here where we have control of everything." And he had us built up, saying, "You guys are the Crickets, you will be the Crickets and you'll keep the Crickets name. And we'll get another lead singer and a guitar player"—so forth and so on. He told us that the Crickets were the ones that had had all the hits—Buddy Holly had only had "Peggy Sue," and he couldn't make a living on the name Buddy Holly. So if we stayed down in Clovis with Norman, we could keep the name the Crickets, and Norman had—quote—"all his money in the bank, and we'll starve him to death"—unquote.

JERRY ALLISON
We sat in the car and went through it all and Buddy was agreeable to the whole thing. He said, "I wish you guys would go with me, you're gonna be sorry you didn't. But I can understand, if you don't want to, you don't want to... Okay, you guys can have the name of the Crickets, and I'll just work as Buddy Holly."

JOE B. MAULDIN
Buddy told us to use the name the Crickets because he wasn't going to use it. He said, "If any of us gets uncomfortable and feels it isn't going to work, all it takes is a phone call to get back together."

MARIA ELENA HOLLY
He felt sort of betrayed... He felt like they had put a knife in his back, but if that was how they felt, he wasn't going to beg them. But he cried that night.

JERRY ALLISON
One of the main reasons that I recall for Buddy splitting was that he wanted more publicity. At the time, people like Fabian and Frankie Avalon were getting all kinds of write-ups in magazines, but Norman didn't believe in that sort of publicity. He told Buddy, "You don't need that—you'll make it on records."

PHIL EVERLY
Boudleaux Bryant wrote "Raining in My Heart" for us and Buddy was in the room when we first heard it. We passed it over to him and he recorded it.

DON EVERLY
That was written for us. Boudleaux gave it to us, but we had an overabundance of material. Buddy was lookin' and said, "I wanna do it," and we said, "Go ahead."

LARRY HOLLEY
The last time I saw Buddy he told me this was going to be his finest song. It was "Raining in My Heart," and he played it and I told him that I really liked it. When I heard it the next time with all that orchestration behind it, I didn't think it was as nice as when Buddy played it for me on his guitar.

NORMAN PETTY
I mentioned strings to [Dick Jacobs] and didn't think he'd want to do it. But he said, "Well, it might really be a pretty keen idea." Since [Buddy] played guitar on our trio record, "Moondreams," he said, "I like that song," which surprised me. So that was going to be one of the songs we'd cut. He said he'd like to do "True Love Ways" and one [that] Boudleaux and Felice Bryant had played for us in Nashville, called "Raining in My Heart." The fourth tune for the session was held open because he'd worked with Paul Anka on an Australia tour, and Paul was writing some songs and wanted to know if Buddy wanted to do any of them. Buddy and Paul got together and decided that they'd do the one called "It Doesn't Matter Anymore." Dick had already done all the other arrangements, so "It Doesn't Matter Anymore" was the last thing we did.

DICK JACOBS
Buddy came into my office at about five o'clock in the afternoon with his guitar, and he said, "Paul Anka just played me the most fantastic song in the world. We have to do it tonight." I said, "Buddy, the session starts in three hours." And Buddy says, "We gotta do it. Please, you gotta write an arrangement. You gotta do it." So I called my copyist—he came right in—and in three hours we had a string arrangement ready on "It Doesn't Matter Anymore," which of course turned out to be the big hit of the session.

WAYLON JENNINGS
He laughed a lot. He believed in simplicity. Like, you can hear those things with the strings on it, "It Doesn't Matter Anymore," and you can tell who arranged it—the syncopation idea I'll bet is his.

DICK JACOBS
We had violins on the date and I had no time to harmonize the violins or write intricate parts, so we wrote the violins all pizzicato... That was the most unplanned thing I have ever written in my life.

PEGGY SUE GERRON (By late 1958 she was Mrs. Jerry Allison.)
They had a full orchestra there. They did not like rock 'n' roll... you could cut the atmosphere with a knife. You could tell that they felt that we were really out of our place. I have to say, thinking back, about Buddy's maturity. He handled that beautifully. He knew what he wanted, he knew why he was there, he worked hard to get there, and he didn't let anybody shake him up.

THE CASH BOX (January 24, 1959)
CORAL 62074............ It Doesn't Matter Anymore / Raining in My Heart Buddy Holly has a pair of winners back to back that could join hands to give him his biggest money-maker since "Peggy Sue." One half, "Raining in My Heart," is a touching romantic lilter from the pen of the Bryants. Infectious side with a clever lyric and a delightful melody. Should get heavy airplay. The companion deck, "It Doesn't Matter Anymore," composed by vocalist Paul Anka, is a refreshing romantic bouncer with a variety of rhythms that immediately arrest the listener's attention. Both sides could make it big.

HENRY GOLDRICH
My wife and I became good friends with Buddy and Maria Elena, and visited their apartment quite often. I know that he had a few tape recorders there that he was using to write songs, and...many guitars.

CAROLYN HESTER (Folk singer who first recorded with Buddy in Clovis.)
One day Buddy called me and said, "There's a rock concert at a theater on Broadway, and my buddy Roy Orbison's there. You wanna go?" I was introduced to Roy Orbison by Buddy Holly—at the time, I didn't realize the impact of it, except that it was fun. I didn't know I'd be surviving all these folks, and it makes me sad now.

RAY CAMPI (Texas rockabilly singer who recorded briefly in Clovis.)
I never met Buddy but I did talk to him once on the phone for about fifteen minutes, right before I recorded for Norman Petty. When I asked him about Norman, he told me, "I'm no longer working with Norman Petty." Buddy's the first one who told me to try and hold on to my song publishing. I sent him a copy of my latest record, "My Screamin' Screamin' Mimi," and I found out many years later that it was part of his personal record collection when he died. Sotheby's, the auction house that handled the sale of Buddy's effects a couple years ago, included "My Screamin' Screamin' Mimi" among his personal record collection that went on the auction block. I hear the record commanded a good price. Finally, a Ray Campi single turns out to be valuable—but only because Buddy Holly owned it!

GEORGE ATWOOD
On January 4th, 1959, a Sunday, Buddy called and said, "I'm down at KLLL, could you come down?" When

I got there, the Corbin brothers and Hi-Pockets were all there. We spoke around, Buddy said, "I'd like to talk to you." He had a cylinder of coffee but we didn't want to drink it. He said, "I'm fixing to go to New York in the morning and I don't really want to go. I'm fixing to build a studio in Lubbock." He knew there was so much talent around town. He'd already ordered a lathe from New York. He had plans drawn up, a studio, offices, loading docks, even apartments for him and Maria. He said, "I want you to be part of my recording team and do the publicity."

MARIA ELENA HOLLY
Norman never believed in advertising or promotion—he never took a page out in *Cash Box* or any of the other big entertainment magazines. "I don't believe in it," is what he'd say... Norman wouldn't even get decent publicity pictures made—he'd take them himself or get his secretary to do it... The first pictures that were suitable for promotion were the Bruno portraits, which I suggested. As soon as we were able to get his money in his hands, we were going to do some real promotion.

NORMAN PETTY
At the time we [NorVaJak] were the copyright owners [of Buddy's songs], that much is true. A company called Melody Lane, one of the off-shoots of Southern Music, had sub-publishing deals, or I should say agency arrangements, with lots of publishers... whereby the company itself owned the copyrights and Southern or Melody Lane would actually collect and disperse all the money, and they would take care of the promotion end of the music publishing operation. Consequently, each writer received a check from NorVaJak, but if they looked closely it really was from Southern Music, the "mother bank" was theirs.

BUDDY HOLLY (In a registered letter to Norman Petty, dated January 8, 1959, asking for the cancellation of his writing contract with Petty's publishing company.)
My lawyer has informed me that he has already gotten in touch with you urging the settlement of the matter... pertaining to my money. I am sure you will do your utmost to bring this matter to a satisfactory climax.

MARIA ELENA HOLLY
Buddy did not have a red cent in his name. Norman controlled all the monies... He paid for everything. Buddy would send him whatever needed to be paid, even the cars that they bought were paid for by Norman. Any money [they] got [they] had to go through Norman.

PHIL EVERLY
I can remember him, one night, playing me all of his songs, and asking me why it was that he couldn't get a hit record. He was so low.

BUDDY HOLLY (Taping a promo for the Winter Dance Party tour in January 1959.)

Hi, this is Buddy Holly. The Crickets and I are really happy to be coming your way on the Winter Dance Party. We certainly hope to see all our old friends and to be making some new ones too. Also, I hope you like my latest Coral release, "Heartbeat." See you soon.

MARIA ELENA HOLLY
The night before Buddy left, I had this dream... Then I woke up, and I must have screamed because I woke Buddy up too. And then he told me about the dream he had been having. He had been dreaming that he was in a small plane with Larry [Holley, who was a licensed pilot] and me. Larry didn't want me to be there but Buddy told him, "Anywhere I go, Maria comes with me." They kept arguing about it and Larry kept landing the plane because he wanted me to get off, and Buddy wouldn't agree, so they'd take off again. Finally, Larry won the argument, and they landed on the roof of a tall building and left me there. And Buddy said, "Don't worry, just stay put—I'll come back and get you." And then he flew off. And that was when he woke up.

TOMMY ALLSUP
He told me he had a tour lined up in January, and he wanted me and Waylon Jennings to back him up. He asked me if I could find a drummer, and I suggested Carl Bunch, who was playing with a rock 'n' roll band in Odessa.

WAYLON JENNINGS
Buddy got me an electric bass and said, "Look, learn how to play this in two weeks." I think I memorized everything he had ever recorded. Anyway, we'd been out on the road for a couple of weeks, and I suddenly realized that the bass strings are just the first four strings of a guitar—you know, from the top down—which really amazed me.

MARIA ELENA HOLLY
I had found out that I was pregnant and I was not feeling very well... That's why I didn't go even though I was planning to.

NIKI SULLIVAN
When Buddy was getting ready to leave on this last tour, he tried to get hold of Jerry, Joe B. and myself by phone from New York. He was unable to contact any of us, I later found out. I returned his call about three days to a week later because I was out and not always in one place at one time.

MARIA ELENA HOLLY
When he went on the tour, Buddy really missed the Crickets—he felt like they added something special to his act. Once when he talked with me on the phone, he said, "If you get a call from Jerry and Joe B., tell them I'll be back in two weeks, and I want to talk to them—alone."

BOB KEANE (Manager/producer of Ritchie Valens.)
Bo Diddley was one of [Ritchie's] favorites, and Buddy Holly. When

you listen to them play guitar, you'll find it's very similar.

TOMMY ALLSUP
It was fun cutting up and singing. We got a great reception; had to turn our amps up full blast to be heard over the screaming. I remember we opened up with "Gotta Travel On" and then we did all of Buddy's hits.

WAYLON JENNINGS
He was used to having Joe B., and all of a sudden he's stuck with me. One night we were playing, and Buddy kept turning around saying something to me, but I couldn't hear him. He did this three or four times, and I'd say, "I can't hear you." Finally he came back and yelled in my ear: "Turn that goddamn bass down!"

DION DiMUCCI (Doo-wop vocalist and leader of the Belmonts who were on the tour.)
We hit it off right away even though, or maybe because we were from such different worlds. I dug Holly's lean, sparse Texas sound and the way he turned out great music on his own terms. But most of all I admired how together he was.

WAYLON JENNINGS
"Gotta Travel On"—Buddy and I worked on that before we left, and another too. He said, "Come here, we're gonna do 'Salty Dog Blues' together." We sang it on the bus, but then we did it onstage at Clear Lake, or the night before. I sang harmony on "That'll Be the Day" and some of Buddy's other songs.

TOMMY ALLSUP
It snowed on us from the time we left Chicago. I don't know why we got such lousy buses, such lousy old buses. Usually the heater wouldn't work.

DION DiMUCCI
There wasn't much to do on that tour bus except to make music and try to keep warm. Back then you didn't have the tricked-out luxury suites on wheels like stars demand today. We were packed into what looked to me like a converted school bus and,

Dion and the Belmonts
Photo: Big Nickel Archives

82

when we got tired, we slept where we were sitting. And when we got tired of that, we'd stretch out in the luggage racks, snoring or just catching our breath in the frigid air. One of the first things that went was the heater. Whenever I hear people talk about the glamour of the rock 'n' roll life, I think of that bus and I have to smile. The new guys—Holly, Ritchie, the Belmonts and I—didn't know any better. We figured this was how it was always done. But the old-timers—players who'd seen a lot of young talent come and go—definitely knew they were hooked up with a third-class operation.

BOB DYLAN
I saw Buddy Holly in Duluth, at the Armory [on January 31]. Buddy was great. Buddy was incredible.

DION DiMUCCI
It was a bitter cold new year with a whole lot of nothing between warm hotel rooms. The bus kept breaking down and it always seemed to happen thirty miles from the nearest town... When that bus would wheeze and shudder to a stop, Holly and I used to climb under a blanket together to keep warm. Through the dark hours while we waited for something to happen, we would tell each other stories. Him, about Lubbock. Me, about the Bronx. I could always get a laugh out of him—soft and low like his drawl... After a couple of hours, someone would start flagging down cars to drive us to the date. Somehow we managed to keep the tour rolling, town after town, and with it, the music. Maybe I was always after someone to look up to, but I remember him as being a lot older than me, even though I was nineteen and he was only twenty-two. He was like Darin, someone you respected. Someone that you learned from and modeled yourself after. And one of the things he taught me—and we all taught each other—was music.

TOMMY ALLSUP
They kept shooting those relic buses up there and we were freezing to death in them. It got so cold that our drummer, Carl Bunch, got frostbite and had to go to the hospital.

DION DiMUCCI
Even though he'd put on six pairs of socks, Holly's drummer came down with frostbitten feet and had to quit the tour. Carlo [Mastrangelo, one of the Belmonts] took over the [drummer's] slot for the rest of the shows. And we got into some friendly competition. Both Buddy and I had the fanciest guitar on the market, the new Fender Stratocaster: mine, pure white: his, with a sunburst on it. We had a little side bet about who could make his ring the longest. To tell you the truth, I don't remember who won.

DOUG McLEOD (Fan who attended the January 30, 1959, show in Fort Dodge, Iowa.)
When Buddy Holly came on, he was of course the last performer. He had his Stratocaster guitar on a guitar rack

on the stage, and it sat there all night long. The others had to play around it. Then, when they introduced him, he came on. The difference between the way he was dressed and the Crickets were dressed is that he had a red ascot with polka dots. Other than that they were all dressed the same, every hair was in place.

BOB HALE (Clear Lake, Iowa, disc jockey and emcee at the Surf Ballroom on February 2, 1959.)
It was the biggest crowd that [ballroom owner] Carroll Anderson had ever had in the Surf—it was the biggest thing I had ever seen. We had people that had driven in from St. Paul, others that had driven in from Illinois and Minnesota. The place was filled to the rafters.

DANIEL DOUGHTERY (Local resident who attended the Surf Ballroom.)
There wasn't dancing while Buddy sang—they all wanted to just listen to him sing. He didn't dance around the stage much, but stayed in one place most of the time. He moved his neck a lot when he sang. He wore a suit with a bow tie and those big, black glasses that made him stand out on the stage. After each song he sang, he got right into another one—he never said hardly a word but "thank you."

DION DiMUCCI
The night before the Fargo, North Dakota, date, he'd worked out a way to get into town early, wash his clothes and get a few hours in a real bed. He'd fly. But he needed some others who would share the charter plane expense and that's what kept me on the bus. It sounded good, but it would cost me $35. That was a month's rent in the old place, a lot of money.

WAYLON JENNINGS
Nobody flipped any coins that I know of. What happened was that Buddy chartered a plane for me, him and Tommy Allsup to fly on. Our bus had frozen up down the road. We were riding this school bus and it was like forty below and a blizzard was coming in that night as a matter of fact... I remember sitting there and Buddy came up and said we would fly. So here comes the Big Bopper and he's got the flu. He came up to me and said, "Waylon, would you mind if I take your place on the plane? I've got to get some rest." He was big and the seats on the bus were small, so he couldn't get any rest. So I said, "It's all right with me if it's all right with Buddy."

MARIA ELENA HOLLY
He told me what an awful tour it had been... He said everybody on the tour was really disgusted with the whole thing. Then he said that the tour was behind schedule and he had to go on ahead of the others to the next stop to make arrangements for the show. He didn't tell me that he was going to fly.

ALAN FREED
That Buddy Holly... If you tied two orange crates together, put a wing on it, and said it would fly, he'd climb in and take off. He always wanted to get someplace ahead of the others.

WAYLON JENNINGS
When I gave up my seat on the plane to the Big Bopper, Buddy came over to me and said, "Well, you're not going to go on the plane tonight?" And I said, "No, Bopper wanted to go." So he says, "Well, I hope your old bus freezes up." And I shot back, "Well, I hope your plane crashes." Imagine how I felt. I was just 20 years old, and I thought I'd caused the accident. It took me two years to get over that before I could go back to making music.

BUDDY HOLLY (Talking to Surf Ballroom manager Carroll Anderson an hour before his flight.)
Well, I'm either going to go to the top—or else I'm going to fall. But I think you're going to see me in the big time.

(right) The Big Bopper bellows "Hello, Baby!"
Photo: BMI/Michael Ochs Archives

(below) Ritchie Valens (right) talks with Jimmy Clanton in the movie *Go, Johnny, Go.*
Photo: Jim Dawson

The crash site, February 3, 1959
Photo: Jim Dawson

Two
"Memories Will Follow Me Forever..."
"That'll Be The Day..."

ROBBIE ROBERTSON (Lead guitarist of The Band.)
The road has taken a lot of the great ones—Hank Williams, Buddy Holly, Otis Redding, Janis Joplin, Jimi Hendrix and Elvis Presley.

THE CLEAR LAKE MIRROR-REPORTER (Clear Lake, Iowa, February 5, 1959)
DEATH OF SINGERS HERE SHOCKS NATION
Rock 'n Rollers, Pilot Die In Tragic Plane Crash

There was no fearful omen of tragedy Monday night when 1,100 teenagers and their parents packed the Surf Ballroom in Clear Lake for a gala "rock 'n roll" dance. Featured were four nationally-known entertainers: Buddy Holly and the Crickets; the "Big Bopper"; Ritchie Valens; and Dion and the Belmonts.

The entertainers were full of pep, reacting joyously to the big crowd of young people. The "Big Bopper" (J. P. Richardson), who wrote the hit song "Chantilly Lace," and Ritchie Valens, author of several top hits, playfully Indian wrestled backstage between acts.

Two hours after the dance, three of the four singers were dead, along with the pilot who was flying them to Fargo, N.D., for another appearance. Their broken bodies were found in and around the wreckage of the light plane they had chartered after the dance Monday night.

Dead were the pilot, Roger Peterson, 21, of Clear Lake; Charles (Buddy) Holly, 22, of Lubbock, Texas; Ritchie Valens (Richard Valenzuela), 17, of Los Angeles, Calif.; J. P. (Big Bopper) Richardson, 28, Beaumont, Texas.

Word of their death when the plane was found Tuesday morning in a snow covered field six miles north of the airport focused nationwide attention on Clear Lake. The three singers are considered among the top rock 'n roll artists in the United States and their recordings are currently on the best selling list, some over the million mark.

The fatal crash occurred on the Albert Juhl farm, in a pasture about a half mile west of the farm house. The plane, a Beechcraft Bonanza chartered from the Dwyer Flying Service, took off about 1 a.m. from the airport with the three men after they were taken to the airport by Carroll Anderson, Surf manager, his wife and son Tommy.

It is believed to have crashed shortly thereafter into the field on the Juhl farm.

Wreckage of the plane was discovered by Jerry Dwyer about 9:30 a.m. Tuesday. He had received no reports from the plane since it departed and he began the search in another plane

Tuesday morning.

The craft first scraped the ground at a spot in the middle of the field, breaking off one wing and other parts of the plane.

It then bounced and skidded about 200 yards further to the northwest, scattering wreckage and debris along the way until it piled into a wire fence along the north end of the pasture.

The plane was completely demolished in the crash, but did not burn.

The bodies of the three entertainers were thrown from the plane, two of them lying a short distance to the south of the plane, and the third [the Big Bopper] was thrown over the fence about 20 feet into the next field.

The body of the pilot was entangled amid the wreckage of the main part of the plane. Ambulances took the victims to the Ward and Wilcox Funeral homes in Clear Lake.

An investigation was launched by the Civil Aeronautics Administration after the crash to determine its cause. Jerry Dwyer, operator of the flying service, could give no reason, stating that the plane was in good condition and that Mr. Peterson was a competent pilot.

Indications pointed to the fact that the plane touched the ground at a low angle, skidding along the field instead of plunging deeply into the ground. The only mark at the place where it first hit was a furrow scraped out by a wing tip.

CAA investigators arrived in Clear Lake later Tuesday and remained overnight. Guards were posted at the scene throughout the day and through Tuesday night to keep the wreckage intact for the investigation.

The major significance of loss of the three artists to the music world was indicated by the immediate requests of national press associations for full coverage. Requests also have been received from *Life* magazine for pictures.

Other members of the troupe who appeared at the Surf Monday night were traveling to Fargo by chartered bus.

Ironically, Buddy Holly had told KRIB disc jockey Bob Hale at the Surf that he didn't want to take a chance in the bus since it had broken down while traveling from Green Bay, Wis., to Clear Lake the day before.

The three therefore decided to charter the plane and take care of advance arrangements in Fargo Tuesday.

BOB BOOE (Mason City resident, disc jockey and friend of pilot Roger Peterson.)
When I got to the airport, I learned that Jerry Dwyer had taken off in a small two-place training aircraft in order to fly along Roger's proposed flight path. About this time we looked out the window of the office of the flight service and saw Jerry returning to the field... We wondered why he was coming back so soon... Jerry taxied in, got out of the Champ, and I could see by the look on his face that something was terribly wrong... Jerry said, "They're in a pas-

ture about five miles from here. I think they're all dead."

LARRY HOLLEY (Besides being Buddy's brother he's a licensed pilot.) I feel like they flew through clouds or a fog and lost visual reference, and [the pilot] got it into the ground before he knew what was happening. An "A" model Bonanza, or any Beechcraft Bonanza with a V tail... if you have the nose down even slightly, it'll pick up speed so fast that you'll be going down before you know it.

BOB BOOE
The airplane appeared to have rolled into a ball, resting up against a fence at one end of the field. In about the center of the field was the left wing of the plane which apparently made the initial contact with the ground and had been torn off. It still lay fairly near the spot where it first struck the ground and started the plane cartwheeling across the ground. In the initial impact, the fuselage of the airplane apparently split open, and the bodies of Ritchie Valens and Buddy Holly were thrown out. They were lying about ten to fifteen feet apart, not too far from the initial point of impact.

CIVIL AERONAUTICS BOARD
(Aircraft Accident Report, dated September 23, 1959.)
A Beech Bonanza, N3794N, crashed at night approximately 5 miles northeast of the Mason City Municipal Airport, Mason City, Iowa, at approximately 0100, February 3, 1959. The pilot and three passengers were killed and the aircraft was demolished.

The aircraft was observed to take off toward the south in a normal manner, turn and climb to an estimated altitude of 800 feet, and then head in a northwesterly direction. When approximately 5 miles had been traversed, the tail light of the aircraft was seen to descend gradually until it disappeared from sight. Following this, many unsuccessful attempts were made to contact the aircraft by radio. The wreckage was found in a field later that morning.

This accident, like so many before it, was caused by the pilot's decision to undertake a flight in which the likelihood of encountering instrument conditions existed, in the mistaken belief that he could cope with en route instrument weather conditions, without having the necessary familiarization with the instruments in the aircraft and without being properly certified to fly solely by instruments.

WAYLON JENNINGS
As weird as it may seem, the next morning when we got to Moorhead, Minnesota, which is fourteen miles away from Fargo, North Dakota... the road manager went into the hotel, and of course they told him what had happened and that the plane had crashed. He came to the door of the bus and said, "Waylon, come outside, I want to talk to you for a minute," and for some reason I said

no. I just said, "No." And he asked me again, "Come on outside," and I said, "No, Tommy, you go," so Tommy Allsup went out. He came back in and said, "Boys, they didn't make it."

DION DiMUCCI
We drove all night and when we got to the hotel, instead of familiar faces and familiar jokes, there were only a couple of old people in the lobby watching a flickering TV in silence. The reporter was talking about a plane crash, interviewing an official who said there were no survivors. I walked back to the bus and sat alone in the cold. All around me were their belongings, with Buddy's starburst Fender propped against a seat. I don't know how long I was there, and I'm not really sure I thought about anything much. No insight. No grief. No comforting words. I was nineteen years old. Death wasn't real.

JERRY ALLISON
Sonny [Curtis] was spending the night. We had been on the road somewhere, and we had been trying to call Buddy the night before. Peggy Sue and I were staying at my folks' house in Lubbock, and Sonny had been sleeping on the living room couch. Sonny woke me up and said, "Hey, man, I've got something real bad to tell you." I couldn't believe it. I thought that there might have been a plane crash and that Buddy might have been around it, but he couldn't be dead, he couldn't possibly be. I had lost my best friend.

SONNY CURTIS
As far as the mood around Lubbock, I really don't think that Buddy was all that famous in his hometown, which was even more of a tragedy. Outside of his parents, friends, and people in the music business, I really don't think it made an impact.

PEGGY SUE GERRON
At first I thought they had made a mistake. I had had a premonition about a month before Buddy was killed. About a plane going up in a snowstorm, going straight up and coming straight down. At this point, I really thought it was Jerry that was in the plane, not Buddy. And I had had that dream over and over and over.

MARIA ELENA HOLLY
[Singer Lou Giordano called and] asked me if I had seen the television or listened to the radio yet, and when I told him I hadn't, he said, "Don't turn them on—I'm on my way over." But I turned on the radio. And my aunt came in just as I heard the news... I was sick in bed that day... The following day I lost the baby.

ELLA HOLLEY
A woman called me and said, "Have you heard the news? There's news about Buddy on the radio." My husband turned it on, and that's how we found out about Buddy.

LARRY HOLLY
I was checking out one of my tile

jobs and my other brother, Travis, was working for me. I hadn't had the radio on that morning. It was a cold day, and I was wandering around checking jobs, wondering where all my people were. My brother wasn't on the job, and I couldn't find anyone. So I went up to a cafe to eat and the lady there said, "That was sure bad about the boys, wasn't it?" And I said, "What boys?" She answered, "Isn't your name Holley?" When I said yes, she replied, "Well, Buddy Holly and them, they had a plane crash."...And I thought, Lord, if you'll just help me, if he's still alive, I'll go up there, I'll fight the elements, I'll do whatever. But it was too late.

NORMAN PETTY
Jerry Allison called me. It was very early on the morning after the crash, right after they had called him. It was a terrible shock.

BOB LINVILLE (Member of the Roses, who sang background vocals on "It's So Easy.")
I woke up about ten that morning. Now, we're talking about 1959, no instant TV, fade in and out, no instant on, you got sound before picture. I turned the TV on in the living room and they said, "Buddy Holly... is dead." Buddy's picture came on the television... I ran over [to Norman Petty's] and busted in. Norman and Vi were both crying in their apartment upstairs.

JOHN PICKERING
I didn't hear about it until I was at work in Corpus Christi about 9:30 a.m. One of my co-worker's wives called him and he told me. I couldn't call my wife to tell her as we couldn't afford a phone. She called me a little later. She'd heard it on the car radio on her way to a church meeting. She was eight months pregnant and very upset. I was numb and felt like crying... My second feeling was anger. Buddy had worked so hard and deserved all the great things that were happening. He hadn't even peaked, and what the hell was he doing in a corn field in Iowa in a snowstorm?

BOBBY VEE (Buddy Holly sound-alike vocalist who recorded a dozen hits in the early 1960s.)
I used to go to all the shows that came through my home area, which is Fargo in North Dakota. I had tickets in the front row for the Buddy Holly show, and I was a big fan. I was a sophomore in high school, in the tenth grade. I came home for lunch and my brother told me of the tragedy as the radio station had been making announcements. The local radio station was promoting the show, and they decided to go ahead with the remainder of the show, which included Dion and the Belmonts, Frankie Sardo and the new Crickets. They wanted local entertainers to fill the evening, and one of the guys in our band rang the station and volunteered our services. We arrived about 6:45 and the show started at 7:30. They told us that we were going on first, and as we were

Buddy Knox
Photo: Jim Dawson

only a garage band, we didn't have a name. I told them that we were the Shadows with a question mark, and that was our first job in front of a large audience. There was a tradition that the show must go on, but both the performers and the audience were in shock.

BUDDY KNOX
I went to see some friends in Regina, Saskatchewan. I started heading back home, I was living in Nashville at the time and I drove into a snowstorm. It was snowing so hard that I couldn't drive, so I holed up in a gas station and kept my car engine and heater running 'cause it was so cold. I went to sleep, and the next day I was driving along in the afternoon when I heard about the three singers getting killed. I pulled over and checked my map, and at the time they crashed I was about thirty miles away. They had been crazy to fly in it. It had been impossible to drive, so imagine what it was like 4,000 feet up. Once they hit that storm, they should have told the kid to land. I'd have said, "If we're going to miss a date, we miss a date."

LARRY WELBORN
I was working with Charlie Phillips... he wrote "Sugartime." I was working with him and we were coming back from Midland [Texas], I think it was, and we heard it on the radio. It was real hard to believe, I just couldn't accept it... I was an honorary pallbearer.

GARY TOLLETT
I was in Lubbock and was still going to Texas Tech University and had just driven to a nine o'clock class. I had the radio on and was listening to the news. There was a news flash that Buddy Holly had just been killed. I just listened in disbelief. I just couldn't believe it. Then I went over and told Romona, she worked at the Physics Department at Tech, and we were in shock.

SHARON SHEELEY (Songwriter of "Poor Little Fool" and girlfriend of Eddie Cochran.)
I was driving to Gold Star recording studios [in Hollywood] to do a demo session. I had pulled out of the apart-

ment and had only gone a couple of blocks when I heard the news on the radio. I swerved over and almost fainted. Eddie and I had just talked to Buddy on the phone a few days before.

DON McLEAN (Singing the lyrics of his number-one 1971 hit, "American Pie.")
"February made me shiver
With the news that I'd deliver,
Bad news on the doorstep,
I couldn't take one more step.
I can't remember if I cried,
When I read about his widowed bride,
But something touched me deep inside,
The day the music died."

SKEETER DAVIS (Country singing star best known for her 1963 hit "The End of the World.")
I loved Buddy Holly. I was a big fan of his. I remember sitting with Ernest Tubb and his band when the tragedy occurred. We were in Iowa [too].

RONNIE MILSAP (Popular country music singing star of the 1970s.)
He sounded so sincere. And he wasn't that much older than I was! It was like being hit with a tow sack full of wet concrete the day they told me that Holly and the others had died. It was like losing a member of the family.

BOB LINVILLE
Phil and Don Everly, Dave Bigham and I were the honorary pallbearers.
You know the picture that was on the front of *The Buddy Holly Story* [LP]? That was the same picture which was on his casket.

MARIA ELENA HOLLY
I was in Lubbock, but I could not attend the funeral. I could not handle that. My reasoning was I didn't want to see Buddy dead. I wanted to keep his memory the way I saw him when he left.

ELLA HOLLEY
We felt a little bit guilty at the time of his death. It's as though we had pushed him into it by encouraging him too much. But we didn't. He wanted it too.

WAYLON JENNINGS
After that I just kind of quit. I went back to radio. Back to Lubbock for a couple of years. I wasn't even interested anymore. It was just such a ridiculous waste.

GEORGE HAMILTON IV
I did tours with Eddie Cochran, Gene Vincent, Buddy Holly and Sam Cooke, and I remembered them as a lot of fun. I had no idea that those people would die so young. I wish I had told them how much I loved them and how much I enjoyed their friendship, but you assume that somebody like Buddy Holly is going to live forever. He was such a powerful personality and you didn't consider that he might die young.

DOUG McLEOD
The tour was to go to Moorhead, Minnesota, that Tuesday night, and they were scheduled into Des Moines at the Val Air Ballroom the following Thursday night [after the crash]. So we went down to that to see what the nature of the show would be like without the stars there. Frankie Avalon was brought in, and it seems Jimmy Clanton was there... I can remember that it was a very emotional evening, what with the Crickets trying to perform all of the Buddy Holly songs on their own without him. They all looked like they were in a deep state of shock.

ROY ORBISON
Elvis Presley was a great admirer of Buddy, whom he considered to be one of the true originals of rock 'n' roll. Although they met only once [sic], when Buddy opened a show for Elvis at the Cotton Club in 1955. Elvis had a complete collection of all his records. And I can tell you that he was pretty shook up when Buddy died so tragically.

MARIA ELENA HOLLY
The only way I got money was when Buddy died and I used my lawyers. I had to use all kinds of methods to be able to get [Norman Petty] to cough it up... Buddy never did recoup all his money.

NORMAN PETTY
It has been said that Buddy and later his wife started legal proceedings against me. That was not so. After Buddy's death, they did hire the attorneys to come down and close out, examine the books, the moneys earned and so forth.

The Walk of Fame Monument in Lubbock, TX (right)
Gravesite (below)

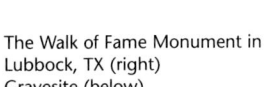

Photos: Jeff Riley

Two

"Memories Will Follow Me Forever..."
"Not Fade Away"

JOHN LENNON
I often wonder what his music would be like now, had he lived.

JERRY LEE LEWIS
One of the most genuine people I knew. He called me up before he got married, and I said, "Do you love the lady?," and he said, "I love her with all my heart." And I said, "If you do, then do it, marry her." He did no pills, no dope, no nothing—he was a perfect dude for people to know.

IAN WHITCOMB (British singer whose 1965 record, "You Turn Me On," was a Top 10 hit.)
The Daily Mirror had the biggest circulation of any daily newspaper in Europe, and when Buddy Holly, Ritchie Valens and the Big Bopper died they made the front page, banner headlines across the top. I understand it wasn't such a big deal in the States. But in England Buddy enjoyed an extraordinary popularity. He was just as popular as Elvis, and still is.

BRUCE WELCH (Rhythm guitarist of the popular British group the Shadows.)
I cried when I heard of his death. I was stunned. I was walking to catch the underground at Finsbury Park station when I saw the front page of *The Daily Mirror*. "Top Rock Stars Die in Crash!" screamed the headline, and there was a picture of the Big Bopper at the top of the page and a smaller one of Buddy Holly below.

TOMMY "SNUFF" GARRETT
(Liberty Records' A&R man.)
In my early days I was a deejay in a town [Wichita Falls] in Texas, and I became acquainted with Buddy Holly. I met Buddy Holly late in 1956... So I knew Buddy for a long time. Then later I went to Los Angeles to become a record producer. Somebody brought me a tape of a boy, and he reminded me of Buddy. He sounded like Buddy to me. So I signed Bobby [Vee] and started recording him. I tried to pick up with him where I thought Buddy might have left off.

BOBBY VEE
My intentions were different than Snuffy's. I was sixteen years old at the time and I think Buddy Holly was my second inspiration after Elvis, and happened to have been my favorite singer at the time, and I was very impressionable. Our band did all the Buddy Holly and the Crickets songs, so it was subliminal as far as I was concerned. There's no question that I sounded like Buddy Holly.

JONATHAN KING (British singer best known for his hit "Everyone's Gone to the Moon.")

I think it was 1958 [sic] when I heard Buddy Holly's "It Doesn't Matter Anymore," late 1958 when I was at Charterhouse, and all of a sudden the whole thing opened up new horizons for me. Beforehand I'd sneered at pop rather like people used to sneer at acting. I suddenly thought, "My god, this is absolutely fantastic," and all the classical music which I was then liking, I threw to one side.

JOHNNY WORTH (Popular British singer-songwriter.)
I can remember standing on the Hungerford Bridge and working out an arrangement for "What Do You Want," and this was before Buddy Holly. I loved the way Tchaikovsky had used pizzicato strings, and I thought, "That's what I'll use if I ever make a record. I'll have a classical sound and it won't be rock 'n' roll." Johnny Kidd tried it as a rock 'n' roll number, but I wasn't going to have it done that way. By the time Adam Faith was going to record it, "It Doesn't Matter Anymore" had been number one and I said to Adam, "Let's do a Holly on it because there's nothing more successful at the moment, especially with his distinctive pronunciation of 'baby.' We'll stick that in." ["What Do You Want" shot to number one in the U.K., and Worth himself recorded a cover of "It Doesn't Matter Anymore."]

FRANK IFIELD
I recorded "True Love Ways" as a dedication to Buddy Holly, and it's the only time I've attempted an impersonation on record. I love all his songs, and that one in particular.

EDDIE COCHRAN (Ad libbing with a throb in his voice on a 1959 tribute song called "Three Stars.")
Buddy Holly, I'll always remember you, with tears in my eyes.

SHARON SHEELEY
Eddie missed Buddy terribly. When

Songwriter Sharon Sheeley with Eddie Cochran
Photo: Jim Dawson

we were on that last tour in England, I found him sitting in his room with the lights turned down low and listening to Buddy's records. I told him, "This isn't good for you, honey, you're only gonna hurt yourself." And then he said in a kind of distant voice that he might be seeing Buddy soon.

PHIL EVERLY (Speaking in 1960, shortly after Eddie Cochran's fatal car crash near London.)
We'll all miss Eddie, just like we miss Buddy Holly. In this kind of business, your friends aren't always people you see every day. They're people you know and you've toured with.

RAY CAMPI
Jerry Green was a singer and country disc jockey in Austin. Right after the plane crash he came to me and said, "Why don't we write some songs about the crash?" I said, "Okay, but I don't want to do anything corny, with angels floating around in heaven. Let's keep it happy and down to earth." We drove down to Pappy Daily's Starday studio in Houston and recorded with the Big Bopper's band. I think we wrote most of "The Ballad of Donna and Peggy Sue" on the way down. I tried to sing like Ritchie Valens and Buddy, and it came out only a couple of days later on Pappy's D label. It was the first tribute record to the three stars. We came out a couple of weeks before "The Three Stars," but it sold a million and we sold, I don't know, maybe a thousand.

DICK JACOBS
He had been a major artist for us and the immediate question from the bosses upstairs was, "What are we going to do for future Buddy Holly material?" Fortunately we had the demo tapes Buddy had left with me and some others that Maria Elena had, so we decided to go into the studio and write arrangements around these things. We hired Jack Hansen and assigned him the job of overdubbing a good rock rhythm section and local studio singers. We were trying to imitate the Crickets... The way we worked was we would put Buddy's tape on one machine, then the musicians—piano, bass, drums and electric guitar—they would all sit with earphones on and we would play the original tape and they would fit their playing to match it. Once we had the rhythm section down we would add the vocal group doing their part, but since this was another overdub, we would lose another generation every time.

BILLBOARD (August 3, 1959)
****Peggy Sue Got Married—CORAL 62134—Follow-up to Holly's big hit. Attractive warbling job on catchy rockabilly-styled item.
****Crying, Waiting, Hoping—The late Buddy Holly sings plaintively on an appealing rockabilly ditty.

JERRY ALLISON
What those people had done with Buddy's last songs—that was awful, Buddy would have hated that stuff.

PHIL EVERLY

From time to time I see girls wearing Buddy Holly T-shirts. Buddy would have loved that sort of notoriety.

DON EVERLY

His was the first musically enclosed group in which the band played and sang and did the whole thing. No one had ever really done that. I think that young kids sitting out there could say, "Well, you play the drums, I'll be the singer, and you be the guitar player and you be the bass player, and we'll be like Buddy Holly and the Crickets."

ROBIN LUKE (Singer-guitarist whose "Susie Darlin'" was a 1958 hit.) Another person who influenced me was Buddy Holly. I had the chance to get to know him, as I remember, on the Dick Clark Saturday show. Buddy and I were backstage for hours. It's hard to explain, but when you're with someone who has been such an influence in your life, and all of a sudden you're sitting in a room alone with him and he is showing you the chord structure to "Peggy Sue" and how he came to play it, it becomes a real special moment.

FATS DOMINO

I don't remember nothin' much about Buddy Holly, but I know I worked with him. But I didn't know he was as big as he was until later. But they talk about Buddy Holly more after he died than they did when he was living. Even though we worked shows together, I didn't pay much attention.

CARL PERKINS

I think Buddy Holly was one of the most talented boys that I had the opportunity to be around. I didn't work that much with him, perhaps two or three tours with him. I found him to be very humble, quiet offstage and in dressing rooms... and a very knowledgeable boy. Buddy had a unique style. It was not a Sun Records sound, but it was full of rhythm and his songs were very good. He was a very talented writer and above all that, he was one of the finest human beings I knew. I never heard him use profanity even in the dressing rooms. Everybody that I know that knew Buddy loved him and you can't have anything ever said better about someone. He was just that sort of fellow. Although he was quiet and subdued in the dress-

Carl Perkins, Columbia Records promotional shot
Photo: Jim Dawson

ing room, when he went onstage he was fire. He did his thing. We lost a lot when we lost him. I feel the music world really took a beating, and I've often wondered for many years now what he would have written and what he would have done.

JIMMY PAGE (Lead guitarist for the Yardbirds and Led Zeppelin.)
Solos which affected me could send a shiver up my spine, and I'd spend hours and in some cases days trying to get them off. The first ones were Buddy Holly chord solos like "Peggy Sue," but the next step was definitely James Burton on Ricky Nelson records, which was when it started to get difficult.

MIKE BERRY (British rocker whose "Tribute to Buddy Holly" was a 1961 hit in the U.K.)
I was weaned on Buddy Holly. I was mad on his songs and I found that I could sing like him, still can. In the early days, we didn't know enough chords to do the songs properly, so we just sang the tune across the wrong chord. The audiences didn't seem to mind.

GEOFF GODDARD (Composer of "Tribute to Buddy Holly.")
I didn't write the tribute with the idea of commercial gain. It was just something I felt like doing. It came out naturally and [record producer] Joe Meek liked it very much. He played it to Mike Berry and one thing led to another. Joe Meek was very interested in the occult and he held a few seances to try and contact Buddy Holly. They were just card and tumbler seances, which is a bit way off mid-stream spiritualism.

MIKE BERRY
Joe Meek said he had been in touch with Buddy Holly and that it was okay to do this tribute. I didn't believe a word of it, but I liked the idea of a tribute to Buddy Holly. I was shattered when he died. The song could have had a better lyric. When I re-recorded it, I changed it from "The snow was snowing" to "The snow was falling," which it does. I was wary of being accused of cashing in on Buddy Holly, but Joe got the Buddy Holly Appreciation Society to give the record its seal of approval.

RITCHIE BLACKMORE (Lead guitarist for the British group Deep Purple.)
Joe Meek was very secretive about the things he did, and he'd tell me that he had been speaking to Buddy Holly, who told him that he must do this record, which was "Tribute to Buddy Holly." He actually thought he could communicate with Buddy Holly.

GEOFF GODDARD
Joe Meek used to say to me, "Play 'Maybe Baby' and that'll get us into the mood." We'd come up with songs like 'Doncha Think It's Time,' which was a good one.

MIKE BERRY
For a while there Joe Meek was one of our biggest record producers, a true genius. He was our Phil Spector.

But he went a little mad, didn't he? I knew he was obsessed with Buddy, but I never dreamt he'd commit suicide on the anniversary of Buddy's death [in 1967].

TONY JACKSON (Bass player of the Searchers.)
When you're learning guitar and you only know three chords, you generally end up playing most of Buddy Holly's stuff. Then you learn a minor chord, which is great, and you can do all of his stuff. He wrote very, very good melodies and "Listen to Me" is one of my favorites. When we recorded it [in 1963], Mike Pender and I sang the lead together, but the talking's me.

BOB DYLAN
When you need somebody to latch onto, you find somebody to latch onto. I did it with so many people, that's why I went through so many changes. I wrote a lot of stuff like Hank Williams, but I never grasped why his songs were so catchy or so classic. As for Presley, I don't know

The Beatles in their 1964 film, *A Hard Day's Night*
Photo: Jim Dawson

1. How did you personally react to The Crickets' tour of England in 1958?

i only saw them on the london palladium (on T.V.)he was great!it was the first time i saw a fender guitar!being played!!while the singer sang!!!also the 'secret'of the drumming on PeggySue was revealed...live...

2. What effect do you think it had on British musicians?

i only know its affect on me.but i reckon the records had the biggest effect on all of us.EVRY GROUP TRIED TO BE THE CRIKETS.
the name BEATLES was directky INSPIRED by CRICKETS(DOUBLE ENTENDRE/INSECTS etc..)
i think the greatest effect was on THE SONG WRITING.(ESPECIALLY MINE AND PAULS)

3. What do you think of Buddy Holly, musically and historically?

he was a great and inovative musician.he was a 'MASTER'.his influence continues.

i often wonder what his music would be like now,had he lived...

4. Do you think his music had any effect on the style of The Beatles? On your own feelings toward music?

see above.we'did'practically every thing he put out.I.E.live at the cavern etc,etc.
what he did with '03" chords made a songwriter out of me!!

5. Other remarks?

he was the first guy i ever saw with a capo.xxxHe made it O.K. to wear glasses!
i WAS buddy holly.

love
John Lennon

In a September 1974 letter to John Lennon, Jim Dawson appended this questionnaire. Within a month, Lennon returned it with his answers typed and marked.
Photo: Jim Dawson

anybody my age that did not sing like him, at one time or another. Or Buddy Holly.

PAUL McCARTNEY
["That'll Be the Day"] was the first record we ever made as the Beatles, in a little studio in Liverpool. We just ran up there one day and made this shellac record.

KEITH RICHARDS
[Holly] passed it on via the Beatles and via us. He's in everybody... This is not bad for a guy from Lubbock, right?

KENNEY JONES (Drummer for the Small Faces, and the late Keith Moon's replacement in the Who in 1979.)
It was like rock 'n' roll picked up more in places like Liverpool. Whereas you came down to London and it was more blues and jazz influences. The Stones were more blues and jazz; they weren't really rock 'n' roll. Suddenly they developed into a rock 'n' roll band. In the sixties in England there were the Mods and the Rockers. The Beatles were Rockers. They'd wear leather and that sort of thing, slick back their hair, and play very fast Buddy Holly stuff. I would say that's where the rock 'n' roll influence came from, and it only slowly came down to London.

GEORGE HARRISON
I'm influenced by Buddy Holly. I mean, right to this day I could play you the "Peggy Sue" solo any time,
or "Think It Over" or "It's So Easy." I knew all them tunes.

JOHN LENNON
We did practically everything he put out, i.e., live at the Cavern, etc., etc. What he did with three chords made a songwriter out of me.

PAUL McCARTNEY
We used to write songs like Buddy. The very first songs that John and I wrote, we used to sag off school and go to my house and sit down with guitars. [Plays a "Peggy Sue" riff on his guitar and starts hiccuping.] And all that. We'd just [say], "How does he do it?" And eventually out of it we got a couple of little songs, we got "Love Me Do," which was the first Beatle record.

BOBBY VEE
I was on tour with my producer Snuff Garrett in the Northwest of England when someone played me "Love Me Do." We loved it and thought it sounded like a Crickets record.

HUEY P. MEAUX (Prolific American record producer.)
The Beatles were a combination of Buddy Holly, Chuck Berry and Bruce Channel—you only have to play "Hey! Baby!" next to "Love Me Do" to see that—the West-Tex sound if you like.

RORY GALLAGHER (Irish rock singer.)
I liked the Beatles a lot, particularly

the way they revived an interest in Carl Perkins and Buddy Holly.

BOB DYLAN
Buddy Holly was a poet. Way ahead of his time. Read his story. I played with Buddy Holly [sic] in North Dakota, South Dakota, ballrooms, youth dances...

JOHN LENNON
The name Beatles was directly inspired by Crickets.

PAUL McCARTNEY
It all came out of this idea of three chords, a group standing up there playing your instruments... you can see echoes of Buddy Holly and the Crickets in the Beatles.

GEORGE HARRISON
Buddy Holly was my very first favorite and my inspiration to go into the music business. I still think he's among the very best. He was different, exciting and inimitable.

TONY BRAMWELL (Boyhood friend of George Harrison.)
I used to lend George all my Buddy Holly records so he could try to learn the various chords and riffs. We played them all so much that by the time we'd finished, they were just about ready for the bin.

GEORGE HARRISON
We looked at fellas like Buddy Holly and Elvis and thought, "That looks like a good job." Money, travel, chicks, nice threads—there's a good deal to be said for playing rock 'n' roll.

PAUL McCARTNEY
We were learning guitars at the time, and Buddy came up and you could watch him, you could actually see that he could play. It was like a guy attraction. Whereas the girls liked Elvis because he looked good, we liked this fellow. He didn't look good, that didn't matter, but he played great.

JERRY ALLISON
Buddy Holly would have loved the Beatles and the Stones and the whole English invasion. He would have kept coming out with stuff because he was always coming up with something new. Just before he died, he was talking about making a gospel album with Ray Charles.

DENNY LAINE (Co-founder of the Moody Blues and guitarist for Paul McCartney's Wings.)
I was listening to Buddy Holly a lot. He was my first real inspiration. In fact, the guitar solo on "That'll Be the Day" made me want to learn to play.

DONOVAN (British folk-rocker best known for such '60s hits as "Mellow Yellow.")
I listened to Buddy Holly and the Everly Brothers. Every week I'd work at the local fruit market selling fruit and reject cakes, and every Saturday I'd take my money and buy an extended-play record of Buddy Holly. The Beatles were influenced by the harmonies of the Everly Brothers. I was solo, so I went for Buddy Holly.

ROY ORBISON
My son goes from one thing to another, but I was amazed that he had *Buddy Holly's Greatest Hits* and that he loved it and wanted to know more about him.

HARVEY ANDREWS (British songwriter who wrote "Don't Get on the Plane.")
All the great songwriters that I personally love—Tom Paxton, Paul Simon, Lennon and McCartney—came from Buddy Holly. When rock 'n' roll started, there was something about Buddy Holly that got to us. He was the first singer-songwriter, although we didn't know it at the time. The B-side of "That'll Be the Day" was "I'm Lookin' For Someone to Love" and one verse goes, "Drunk man, street car, foot slipped, there you are," nine words, and it's lyric writing at the very highest level. That's a book, a novel, a play and a film. We didn't know it at the time, but he was influencing all of us. You check with other songwriters. We don't go back to Little Richard, we don't go back to Fats Domino, we don't go back to Elvis, though we liked all of them. Buddy Holly was the one that the young songwriters could relate to.

ELVIS COSTELLO (Bespectacled British new wave artist often compared visually with Buddy Holly.)
Someone who lived across the road from my grandmother liked Buddy Holly. I thought that was terribly old-fashioned. I couldn't understand why anybody liked it.

PETE TOWNSEND (Lead guitarist of the Who.)
Rock 'n' roll itself lasted as long as the pundits said it would—a couple of years. I mean, Elvis only made one rock 'n' roll album. Then there were a couple of albums from Bill Haley and one from Eddie Cochran. Buddy Holly isn't really rock 'n' roll at all, but you'd concede one album.

ALLAN CLARKE (Lead singer of the British rock group the Hollies.)
We were doing a gig one night in late 1962, and we were looking at the possibilities of getting a good name because we had a feeling that things were going to happen. Because it was near Christmas and we were fans of Buddy Holly, we called ourselves the Hollies.

BOBBY ELLIOTT (Drummer of the Hollies.)
Just before "Long Cool Woman in a Black Dress," Allan would do a throwaway version of "Peggy Sue." It always went down well and Tony suggested that we do an album of all Buddy Holly material. We produced it ourselves and we were pleased with the end product. But true Buddy Holly supporters didn't like the way we rearranged the songs.

JIM REESE (Lead guitarist of the West Texas group the Bobby Fuller Four.)
Bobby [Fuller] was a great imitator. He could sing just like Holly, McCartney, Lennon or Eddie Cochran. And he could imitate on the guitar too. But Bobby never did

Bobby. To me, the overwhelming impression I get from his singing is Buddy Holly, as well as his guitar playing, with a lot of Dick Dale and a smattering of Chuck Berry.

BOB KEANE (Record company owner who produced the Bobby Fuller Four.)
We got into ["Let Her Dance"] and [Bobby] was doing it just like a copy of Buddy Holly. I said, "Buddy Holly is Buddy Holly! Even if you're better than Buddy Holly"—which he probably was, with the technology change—"you've got your own thing going here. Let's try something new."

MARSHALL CRENSHAW (Rock artist who portrayed Buddy Holly in the 1987 film *La Bamba*.)
I don't sound that much like him, and I don't look that much like him. It just so happened that I've always loved Buddy Holly, and I can't help it. I really identify with that music so strongly.

WAYLON JENNINGS
After Buddy died, we were playing at a club in Phoenix called JDs, and we were like the hottest thing there; a good crowd every night and standing room only on the weekends. So one night I said to [drummer] Richie [Allbright], "Well, I think it's time to leave." And Richie said, "Leave? With this kind of crowd really digging what we're doing?" I said, "Yep. That's one thing I learned from Buddy. If you leave now, when you're ahead, they'll exaggerate how good it was. But if you wait till it's all over, when you're starting to lose it, they'll exaggerate how bad it was."

SONNY CURTIS
I'll tell you what, a lot of people try to imitate Buddy's playing and they can't do it. I've been playing his songs every night for 20 years and I've got them down pretty close to the way I think he played them, but I'm still guessing. Like "Rock Me My Baby," I still can't figure out how he did that.

JERRY ALLISON
We've pretty well proved in the years since 1958 that the Crickets without Buddy Holly aren't too hot an item.

GORDON WALLER (Half of the 1960s British duet, Peter & Gordon, whose remake of Buddy's "True Love Ways" was a Top 10 American hit.)
Of the two of us, Peter [Asher] was the folk singer and I was the rock 'n' roller, the Buddy Holly fan. It was a good combination. Recording "True Love Ways" was my idea, really, because it was a fantastic song.

PETER ASHER (The other half of Peter & Gordon, and later Linda Ronstadt's producer.)
Buddy Holly was one of my favorites as a writer and singer. He was even more popular in Britain than here, and still has a huge cult following in England.

LINDA RONSTADT
I had been doing "That'll Be the Day" in concert appearances long before I

finally recorded it. Peter [Asher] thought that we ought to include it on the next album [*Hasten Down the Wind*]. When it became a hit, we included "It's So Easy" on *Simple Dreams*. I wasn't familiar with that one, but Peter was.

DON McLEAN (Singer-songwriter who declared February 3, 1959, as "the day the music died.")
Buddy Holly was the unsung and unnoticed genius of rock 'n' roll for 20 years before being discovered in the '70s... He was a genius and every bit as important as Elvis Presley. It is obvious to me and to everybody who loves Buddy Holly that rock 'n' roll would not be the same without him.

BOB DYLAN
The music of the late fifties and early sixties when music was at that root level—that to me is meaningful music. The singers and musicians I grew up with transcend nostalgia—Buddy Holly and Johnny Ace are just as valid to me today as then.

MADDY PRIOR (Member of the British vocal group Steeleye Span, who recorded an acappella version of "Rave On.")
I was brought up on Buddy Holly, great stuff, and it doesn't date for me at all.

LES GRAY (Lead singer of the British group Mud.)
We stole the idea for "Oh, Boy!" completely from Steeleye Span. We loved the way they did "Rave On" and we wanted to do something as a relief from all the rock 'n' roll we were recording for an album. I remember being on a roundabout, and we started singing "Oh, Boy!" instinctively knowing what all our parts were. We had finished our deal with Rak [Records] and [producer] Mickie Most said, "'Oh, Boy!' is going to be your last single." I said, "You're trying to murder us just because we're leaving. That's not a single, it's just a change [of pace] on the album." It was released on a Friday and the following Tuesday it was number two and the next week it was number one [on the British charts, in 1975]. Mickie Most knew a wee bit more about the business than I did.

BILLY SWAN (Singer-songwriter best known for his 1974 hit "I Can Help.")
When Elvis and the Sun stuff came out—Jerry Lee, Carl Perkins and those guys—I think that kinda pulled me toward it a little more. Buddy Holly was another one I really liked. I think that's when I decided I wanted to [go into music].

ERIC CLAPTON
There was a funny Saturday-morning radio program for children, with this strange person, Uncle Mac. He was a very old man with one leg and a strange little penchant for children. He'd play things like "Mule Train," and then every week he'd slip in something like a Buddy Holly record or a Chuck Berry record.

ELTON JOHN
I only needed specs for reading, but as a result of wearing them all the

time to try to look like Buddy [Holly] I became genuinely nearsighted.

JANIS JOPLIN (Interviewed in 1970 on an early news/personality TV show, *First Tuesday*.)
People like Buddy Holly and Leadbelly, they had soul. They'll never die.

BERT WEEDON (British guitarist who recorded the original "Apache" and wrote a famous *Play in a Day* instruction book.)
Buddy Holly was one of the first to use a Fender Stratocaster. Before that, guitars were hollow and this was the first solid guitar. It had a particular sound all of its own, and while Buddy Holly wasn't a brilliant player, he was certainly a good one and he could get a lot out of his instrument. Thousands of boys and girls started to play the guitar because of him.

ERIC CLAPTON
Buddy Holly had been a very big early influence, particularly the way he looked, and I loved the look and sound of his Strat.

HANK MARVIN (Lead guitarist of the seminal British rock instrumental group the Shadows.)
The first time I actually saw a Stratocaster was on the cover of the first Crickets album, *The Chirpin' Crickets*, and Buddy Holly was holding a sunburst Strat. To see a guitar that shape in 1957 was amazing. Bruce Welch and I were in the same skiffle group in Newcastle at the time and we looked at this and thought,

"What on earth is that?"

BRUCE WELCH (Rhythm guitarist of the Shadows.)
We admired Buddy Holly not only for his marvelous songs, but for the way he sang them, in that unusual, jerky, hiccuping style, with his childlike phrasing. He just sounded like no one else. Then there was his guitar. It was Buddy Holly who introduced us to the magnificent Fender Stratocaster. We'd seen nothing like it before—it looked like a spaceship and was way ahead of its time. It became the distinctive symbol of rock 'n' roll.

RORY GALLAGHER
I was a huge Buddy Holly fan, and a Hank Marvin fan as well, of course. He showed this [Stratocaster] to me, and said, "Do you wanna buy it?"

GEORGE HARRISON
If I'd had my way, the Strat would have been my first guitar. I'd seen Buddy Holly's Strat, I think, on *The Chirpin' Crickets* cover, and tried to find one, but in Liverpool in those days the only thing I could find resembling a Strat was a Hofner Futurama.

BRIAN POOLE (Lead singer of Brian Poole & the Tremeloes.)
At one stage there was nothing in our act that wasn't a Buddy Holly song. We hadn't seen a Fender Stratocaster before—this was like a flat plank and now every guitar is like it. We were so much into Buddy Holly that I had the hair and the glasses exactly like him.

BO DIDDLEY
At the time I thought the Rolling Stones had ripped me off when they recorded "Not Fade Away." I didn't find out until sometime later that it was a Buddy Holly song and he was the one responsible. I just wish I'd heard his version while he was alive. I'd have told him something.

MARIANNE FAITHFUL (British singer and fabled girlfriend of Mick Jagger.)
Buddy Holly, the Everly Brothers, Chuck Berry. I remember hearing "Not Fade Away" in the coffee bar and wondering what sort of person had written that.

IAN McLAGAN (Pianist of the British group the Faces, formerly the Small Faces, of "Itchycoo Park" fame.)
I've always liked the Stones' version of "Not Fade Away," but the original is beautifully subtle. There's so much left out, it's hard to believe. The drum sound isn't the greatest in the world, but it's perfect for the number. A lot of times, when we've been recording in hotel rooms, Ken [Jones] used a phone book on his lap and it's sounded like that. There aren't enough productions like that these days—there are too many tracks and too many Dolbys and such like.

PAUL McCARTNEY
It was Linda's father's [Lee Eastman] idea to buy a catalog of music for a future investment, so when he asked me what artist's catalog I wanted to purchase, I immediately said, "Buddy Holly."

DON McLEAN
I wrote the opening part of "American Pie" up in my little room where I used to compose. I started thinking back to when I was a paper boy, one of those experiences about growing up in New Rochelle, where I cut open this paper bundle and saw that Buddy Holly, the Big Bopper and Ritchie Valens had been killed. I stood there and couldn't believe it. Holly was my favorite performer. So I started writing, "A long, long time ago," but I didn't know what to do with it. Then I came up with the chorus, which was kind of catchy, but I left the thing alone for three months until finally one day I wrote this whole story about the day the music died. The first time I played it I was opening for Laura Nyro at a concert in Philadelphia. I had a lady come out of the audience to hold the lyrics because the song was very long. People didn't know what the hell I was singing about and I didn't get a very good reaction. The record is where the song happened. This piano player named Paul Griffin, who had worked with Bob Dylan, started running "American Pie" down, and he played the ass off that song. It just started bouncing all over the place. He really pumped the thing and drove it. And with my guitar in his ear and him jumping around on piano, it came together. Once I put the vocal on, it became a very hot record.

JOE ELY (Lubbock singer-guitarist.)
Before Buddy became the biggest

thing out of Lubbock, the city was famous for its UFO visitations. People saw strange lights over Lubbock, it made the national news. Later on we used to wonder if Buddy hadn't been one of the aliens. How else could you explain Buddy Holly in Lubbock, Texas? Maybe he flew in on a flying saucer.

STEVIE RAY VAUGHAN (Texas blues guitarist killed in a 1990 Wisconsin helicopter crash.)
It's a tradition back in Texas, if you're in Lubbock you stop over at the cemetery there where Buddy Holly's buried. He's got this headstone on the ground with a guitar carved on it. You push the last [guitar] pick you used into the dirt next to the headstone. If you go there you'll find all kinds of picks pushed down into the dirt.

PHIL OCHS (Introducing a medley during a concert at Carnegie Hall, March 27, 1970.)
Hi, I'm Phil Ochs, and I'd like to sing some songs that are just as much Phil Ochs as anything else. I'm going to do a group of songs here, now, first recorded by somebody I hold very dear to my heart, from the 1950s, who formed part of my musical mind... He formed a part of my musical mind which wrote "I Ain't Marching Anymore" and "Changes." That kind of thought process came from certain people. And this is one of them. His name is Buddy Holly. He died at an early age in a plane crash. These are a collection of his songs I memorized as a kid and rememorized here. I'd like to do some of them for you.

SKEETER DAVIS (Country singer who recorded a 1967 album called *Skeeter Davis Sings Buddy Holly*.)
Felton Jarvis was producing me because Chet [Atkins] was sick, and I mentioned my love of Buddy Holly. Waylon Jennings was there and we all started talking about [making a tribute album] and the next thing you know, we were doing it... We called up the Holleys and they came to the session. It was so nice meeting them and hearing all about Buddy. But [disc jockeys] wouldn't play the album... I had learned that my fans were all fussed because they wanted me to be on the cover [instead of Holly]... When I go to England I always get people knocking on my door, and it's always Buddy Holly fans who started liking me because of that.

DON McLEAN
"American Pie" became a tool to resurrect the memory of Buddy Holly and get it on track. It's growing all the time.

PHIL EVERLY
I think music [in the mid-'80s] has moved toward us. Look at it like a diagram. You have Buddy Holly, who could reach men in music, people who just like music, you know. Then you had us with the harmonies and Buddy had this guttiness, realness. It's moved towards us. Holly would be a giant if he were alive today.

REX REED (*New York Daily News* critic writing about the film *The Buddy Holly Story* in 1978.)
[Buddy Holly was] that enigmatic teen idol who confounded rock 'n' roll, then died in a plane crash after landing 45 hits [sic] on the charts. He wore ugly horn-rimmed glasses and

Actor Gary Busey in *The Buddy Holly Story*
Photo: Jim Dawson

twitched his way across the stage like a spasmodic, electrocuted flea, with two cretins called the Crickets behind him... [His] songs can hardly be classified as music and are hardly worth making a movie about.

VINCENT CANBY (*New York Times* theater and film critic.)
It's Gary Busey's galvanizing solo performance that gives meaning to an otherwise shapeless and bland feature-length film about the American rock-and-roll star who was killed in a plane crash in 1959. The film... was made with the cooperation of Holly's widow, Maria Elena Holly, and may be a demonstration of why keepers of the flame are not the best people to have around when you're making a movie.

CHET FLIPPO (*Rolling Stone* music and film critic.)
The Buddy Holly Story now stands as the official version of his life, but the movie does not seem to be about the real Buddy Holly.

GARY BUSEY
The first priority when I went in to do the part was that they were going to do the music live, and I've been a musician all my life, and I go, "Uh-huh!" I couldn't believe it, I thought [the producers] were full of shit, they did not know what they were doing, [but] next day I get a call, they say, "Let's go over, they want to record your voice... They want you to go into Village Recorders in Los Angeles." When we got there, nobody had the lyrics to "That'll Be the Day." But being from Oklahoma and being a student of nonsense lyrics, I did some nonsense syllables, and next day we made the reference [tape], and they asked me, "Do you wanna play Buddy Holly?" I thought about it for about five seconds. Nobody had any idea what they were doing.

MARIA ELENA HOLLY (In 1978, after the premiere of *The Buddy Holly Story*.)
Gary Busey came through so vividly. It seemed like Buddy was inside him.

GARY BUSEY
I grew up with Buddy Holly records. I've been preparing unconsciously for fifteen years, and there was no academic approach or any idea about mimicking. In fact, I ended up singing all the songs in the same key Buddy wrote 'em in. Some friends did my bio-rhythms with Holly's and they're the same, and there's a lot of similarities in our demeanor and rhythm, and his philosophies I share in terms of getting things done, so there wasn't so much of a challenge that way.

MARIA ELENA HOLLY (Years later.)
Oh [Gary Busey] is good, for what he's trying to do. But he's just not Buddy.

ELLA HOLLEY
We never did see a script. We just took their word for it that we were going to like it. I guess we were kind of stupid, huh?

LARRY HOLLEY
Forget about that movie completely. Put it completely out of your mind. That movie was completely erroneous. We were very disappointed in it... I don't look at it anymore.

JERRY LEE LEWIS
Gary Busey did the movie, but he didn't get close to Buddy. Like Dennis Quaid could never be Jerry Lee Lewis. That film was junk.

GARY BUSEY
Anthropologists will look at this movie 200 years from now and see a piece of American musical culture, and how an awareness pattern happened indirectly: How Buddy Holly caused long hair and a guitar on every corner.

DOUG FIEGER (Leader of the late '70s power-pop group the Knack, known for "My Sharona.")
I couldn't believe it. You'd think they'd at least get the guitars right. But Buddy had a '70s Telecaster early in the movie, and in the big concert at the end he was playing a 1969 Strat. I mean, the guy was definitely ahead of his time, but in 1959 he did not have a '69 Stratocaster!

SONNY CURTIS
The movie *The Buddy Holly Story* wasn't true to life. For one thing, there are no mountains in Lubbock. It depicted Buddy's parents as being opposed to him doing rock 'n' roll, but not only were they 100% behind Buddy, they were 100% behind all us boys. They were real good people, they were great and they loaned us the car all the time. The movie also portrayed Buddy as a sloppy dresser and Buddy was not like that at all, man. He always had tapered, crisp jeans and moccasins. Nice-looking glasses, too. He always looked as though he'd stepped out of the band-

box. They didn't even acknowledge that I existed or even Norman Petty. The worst thing was depicting J.I. as a racist. That was a terrible thing to do when it wasn't true at all.

NORMAN PETTY
I felt like a nonentity, like some very important years of my life had just been wiped out.

STEVE RASH (Director of *The Buddy Holly Story*.)
It's my understanding that Norman wouldn't give [the producers] permission to use his name unless he had creative control over the script, and that was a no-no.

JERRY ALLISON
They didn't have the rights to use our names in *The Buddy Holly Story*, so they called me Jesse and Joe B. was Ray Bob. Apart from that, I hated it. Nobody who was involved in it knew what really happened.

MICKEY GILLEY (Popular singer-pianist whose version of "True Love Ways" was a number-one country hit in 1980.)
[A Dallas] deejay was really a Buddy Holly fan, and he said that there was something about the song that always caught him. He discovered that they were in the same key and basically in the same tempo, so he's got me and Buddy singing ["True Love Ways"] together, and at the time it was really eerie to me.

GORDON PAYNE (Former lead singer of the Crickets.)
"T-shirt" was the winner in a Write a Song for Buddy Holly Week contest and we were given it to record. It really fits what the Crickets is today [1988]. We had omitted the bridge but, when we told Paul [McCartney, the song's producer] in the studio, he said, "Put the bridge on the front, slow it down and play it with open chords," and that really made it work for us. We ran through it once and then the next time we put it on record. Paul said, "That sounds like the Crickets."

CHARLES WHITE (a.k.a. Dr. Rock, British disc jockey and author of *The Life and Times of Little Richard*.)
What is interesting to me is how all of Buddy Holly's recordings have improved with age. I like him much more now than I did then.

SEYMOUR STEIN (Record industry executive who discovered Madonna and k.d. lang.)
The first time I saw [k.d. lang] she almost looked like Buddy Holly in drag.

BRUCE SPRINGSTEEN
I sing "Rave On" before going out onstage. It keeps me honest.

PAUL YOUNG (Member of the '80s British rock group Mike + the Mechanics.)
I was a huge fan of Buddy Holly and the Crickets when I was a kid. I like some records better than others—

"Peggy Sue" of course—but I liked so much of his stuff. I loved his strange Southern, Texan drawl, and his guitar sound was so different. He must have been one of the first guys to use strings in rock 'n' roll... I was very upset the day he died, and he still influences my music today.

ALBERT LEE (Popular British guitarist who recorded with the Crickets in the early '70s.)
Buddy gave Sonny Curtis one of his jackets. Sonny gave it to me when we drove to Nashville. I was at his parents' house and I don't think his mother was very pleased about it. She'd been looking after the jacket for years and all of a sudden, this stranger walks in and Sonny gives him the jacket.

ALVIN STARDUST (1970s British singer who had several major U.K. hits.)
One of the questions in this market research was, "What do you think about Alvin Stardust doing a ballad?" and it was 98% response of "No way, it won't work." When we recorded "I Feel Like Buddy Holly," my new label Chrysalis said, "Oh, we like that, it's a single," and I knew I mustn't tell them about the research. It might have blown the deal.

BUDDY KNOX
Lee Jackson is a songwriter from Lubbock, and he asked me if I'd like to do "I Named My Little Girl Holly." I changed the melody to fit my style and cut it in Lubbock in a studio right next to the Buddy Holly statue.

WAYLON JENNINGS
Somebody asked me the other day why Buddy Holly has lasted so long when his career was so short, and if you think about it, he was the first writer/singer of rock 'n' roll and he was the only one who came up with anything original after Elvis Presley. Buddy had his own sound and his own style.

BUDDY KNOX
When I'm on the road doing shows, I'm always asked if I remember Buddy Holly and can we do some of his songs... Yes, I remember Buddy Holly and I do play his songs at all my shows.

FATS DOMINO (At the first induction ceremony of the Rock and Roll Hall of Fame in January 1986.)
I wish [fellow-inductees] Buddy, Elvis and Sam Cooke could be here to enjoy what's happening.

RICK NELSON (Talking about Buddy Holly's plane crash, not long before his own death in 1985.)
Boy, that must be a terrible way to die.

MARTY STUART (Country recording artist who once played guitar for Johnny Cash.)
We were talking about Buddy Holly's glasses, about how some farmer found the glasses after the crash. Rick [Nelson] was laughing, and he was talking about how [his own] plane

used to belong to Jerry Lee [Lewis]. But I was thinking how rickety I felt on it.

RICK NELSON (After singing his final song, "Rave On," at his last concert December 31, 1985.)
Rave on for me!

RONNIE MACK (California rockabilly and country artist, best known for his 1986 underground hit, "I Love Traci Lords.")
I worked with Rick Nelson right before he died. He said he'd met Buddy Holly when Buddy came out to Los Angeles, and I think as time went by he appreciated Buddy more and more. I know he always played a couple of Buddy's songs, mainly "Rave On" and "True Love Ways." Rick did the best "True Love Ways" ever. I include it in my act now, and I always sing it the way Rick sang it, with a folkish flavor, which was way different from the way Buddy sang it.

JAMES INTVELD (Los Angeles actor and rockabilly revivalist, as well as the voice of Johnny Depp in John Waters' 1990 cult classic, *Cry-Baby*.)
Buddy Holly died before I was born. I was about ten years old when I first saw an old clip of Buddy on an *American Bandstand* TV special, singing "Peggy Sue." He had wild eyes under these glasses, and he looked frantic and fragile. It scared me so much that I had nightmares about him. Later on, when I was in high school, *The Buddy Holly Story* changed my life. Seeing just three musicians making such wonderful music inspired me. I immediately formed my own band, the Rockin' Shadows, which was a trio just like Buddy Holly and the Crickets. I sang and played guitar, and my younger brother Ricky, who was fifteen, played drums. We could play about 20 Buddy Holly songs note for note. It was pure magic. His songs were melodic, but not too complicated, and so by taking all the mystery out of song writing, they inspired me to start writing songs of my own. I always felt bad about Buddy dying in that plane crash. I felt such empathy for his family too. I never thought I would later experience the same tragedy when my brother was killed in the Rick Nelson crash.

JEFF "SKUNK" BAXTER (Guitarist for Steely Dan and the Doobie Brothers.)
Buddy Holly was a little bit more of a—it was a little sweeter kind of rock 'n' roll.

NANCI GRIFFITH (Folk-flavored Texas country singer-songwriter.)
Buddy Holly is such a hero of mine. I always wanted to grow up and be a Cricket. Nobody played Stratocaster like Buddy or Sonny [Curtis], they had just enough West Texas dirt underneath their fingernails. There was something about the way they played that made it special.

MARY CHAPIN CARPENTER (Popular Grammy-winning country singer-songwriter.)
What is most striking about Buddy

Holly's legacy is the combination of lyrical innocence and the redemptive power of his music—to this day they define what is magic to me about rock 'n' roll.

GRAHAM NASH (Member of both the Hollies and Crosby, Stills and Nash, who helped overdub Buddy's home recording of "Peggy Sue Got Married" with a modern arrangement in 1996.)
It was an exciting yet spooky thing to be doing with someone who has been dead for 37 years, but I believe that we have helped to propel Buddy's music further into the future and it was an honor to be able to "pay back" for the pleasure he has given to all of us.

TONY HICKS (Guitarist of the Hollies.)
The original idea was just to do a Buddy Holly track ourselves. Then Graham rang me one evening and said, "I have this track with Buddy. What do you think?" It all fell into place... [Hollies' keyboardist] Ian Parker then put a different chord structure behind the melody. I got together with him and did a few changes from that. Also, it wasn't in any particular key because there were no guitar tuners in those days. It was just short of A flat. We decided to move that up to A, which improved it. Also, it was slightly out of time because Holly was just strumming away with himself... And in the middle of all this, Graham Nash arrived from the States, just as I was finishing the guitar parts. That just left us to do our side of the vocals with Graham, Allan Clarke and myself. We did it in a day-and-a-half at Abbey Road Studios.

STEVE RIPLEY (Guitarist of the '90s country-rock group the Tractors.)
A long time ago I came to believe that when Buddy recorded, not only was he playing electric guitar through an amp and that sort of thing, but they also put a microphone on his electric guitar. This was in the '50s, and the guitar itself was so disengaged from the sound, so they miked his guitar acoustically. I've been doing that on most everything I do ever since I read that.

LEVON HELM (Drummer-singer of The Band.)
I always thought of it as Buddy Holly and the Crickets, never just Buddy Holly. Working with the Crickets was the most fun I can remember.

ROSIE FLORES (Texas-born queen of '90s rockabilly.)
When I was a small child in San Antonio, Holly came into my life through the "Peggy Sue" single. My older brother played it over and over again till I had memorized every nuance of his vocals. Buddy Holly still makes me wanna sing and play guitar.

PAUL HIPP (Actor who portrayed Buddy Holly in the London and Broadway play, *Buddy*.)
We had a party after the first night of *Buddy* [in 1989] and about one in the morning, someone came in with the

first edition of *The Sun*. It had the headline, *"Buddy* Brilliant,*"* so we knew we were off to a good start.

BILL MILLER (Professional collector, recalling Sotheby's June 23, 1990, auction of Buddy Holly memorabilia.)
I was prepared to spend $1,500 (nearly twice the low estimate) for a signed check of Holly's, but lost it to another bidder willing to pay $3,000! A few minutes later, I, along with the crowd in New York, three thousand miles away, gasped in amazement when lot 408, Holly's Gibson acoustic guitar, came up for bids. My Sotheby's phone rep was very professional and cordial, but even she said "amazing!" and "oh my gosh!" when the bidding went "$35,000...$50,000...$75,000... $100,000...$125,000...and finally ended at a stellar $225,000"—plus the 10% buyer's premium. Unknown to me was the fact that the bidder was none other than the actor who portrayed Holly in *The Buddy Holly Story*, Gary Busey.

PETER DOGGETT (Editor of *Record Collector* magazine.)
After Elvis Presley, Buddy Holly is easily the most collectable artist of the rock 'n' roll era and he's in the Top 10 of most collectable artists of all time.

JERRY ALLISON
The postcards Buddy wrote to his family are fetching crazy prices in these auctions... I don't have a lot of stuff myself, but I do have a signed copy of the first single, "Blue Days, Black Nights," and also a letter that the Beatles wrote to us in 1963, and all four of them signed it.

BILL MILLER
The sale had a very strong finish. A pair of Holly's trademark eyeglasses, estimated at $6,000 to $8,000, went through the ceiling and ended up bringing $41,000. The final lot, Holly's Fender Stratocaster, brought $100,000 against an estimate of $60,000.

MARIA ELENA HOLLY
I have a second pair of his glasses— the ones found in the crash. I treasure everything that belonged to him.

JERRY ALLISON
People think we're still trying to live off Buddy Holly... Sometimes, when I look at all those old photographs of Buddy and us when we were 17 and 18, I think that what we're doing right now [carrying on as the Crickets] is silly. We should cut it out and stay on the farm, but when we get together it's still fun. I guess we have to own up... we're still trying to recapture our youth.

WAYLON JENNINGS
Someone once asked me where I thought music would've taken Buddy. I said, "You're asking the wrong question. Where was Buddy gonna take music?"

BILLY STULL (Manager of Norman Petty Studio in the early 1990s.)
They just show up. Since they've

come so far, sometimes from Europe or even South America and Japan, I can't just turn 'em away, so I usually give 'em a little tour.

BOBBY VEE
I have thought for years that Buddy Holly made some of the best records from that period. The records that he and Norman Petty made were light years ahead of the competition... Buddy Holly recorded so few songs during his short career and I've never heard one that I didn't like.

BRITISH PRIME MINISTER JOHN MAJOR (Asked by the *London Daily Mirror* to name the one record he'd take to a deserted island.)
"Peggy Sue."

PAUL KRASSNER (Humorist, social gadfly and editor of *The Realist*.)
Cut to 1978. Bob Weir looked up at the Great Pyramid and cried out, "What is it?"
   Actually, it was the place for locals to go on a cheap date. The Pyramids were surrounded by moats of discarded bottle caps. The Grateful Dead were scheduled to play on three successive nights at an open-air theater in front of them, with the Sphinx looking on. An air of incredible excitement permeated the first night. Never had the Dead been so inspired. Backstage, [Jerry] Garcia was passing along final instructions to the band: "Remember, play in tune."
   The music began with Egyptian oudist Hamza el-Din, backed up by a group tapping out ancient rhythms on their 14-inch-diameter tars, soon joined by Mickey Hart, a butterfly with drumsticks; then Garcia ambled on with a gentle guitar riff, then the rest of the band, and as the Dead meshed with the percussion ensemble, basking in total respect of each other, Weir suddenly segued into Buddy Holly's "Not Fade Away."
   "Did you see that?" Ken Kesey said. "The Sphinx's jaws just dropped!"

HOWARD STERN (Radio's "king of all media," explaining why he didn't want to fly out of Cleveland during a blizzard after a December 1995 book signing.)
I'm not Buddy Holly. I didn't have to get to the next gig.

ANN RICHARDS (Then governor of Texas, in a 1994 letter.)
Texas is blessed with an amazing diversity of musical styles. Its impact on the American soundscape cannot be denied. With a legacy that includes such seminal artists as Buddy Holly, Van Cliburn, Ornette Coleman, T-Bone Walker, Bob Wills, Janis Joplin and Don Santiago Jimenez, it's easy to see why you can't hear American music without hearing Texas.

LARRY HOLLEY
Of one thing I am certain, the greatest single day in Buddy's life was not when he got his first record out, or went to England, or got married. It was when he realized as a young boy that he was not perfect and was getting into all kinds of jams, when he

trusted in the Lord as his Savior and became one of God's children... Anyway, the Lord took him on a little early, and I am sure he had his reasons.

MARIA ELENA HOLLY
Now I've come to accept that it was just meant to be. And I have my memories—there's not a day goes by I don't think of Buddy. I have never really gotten over him.

ELLA HOLLEY
When he died, there was a numbness. Each year we thought, well, this is the end of it, but each year it has gone on.

BUDDY HOLLY (Writing in 1953.)
Well, that's my life to the present date, and even though it may seem awful and full of calamities, I'd sure be in a bad shape without it.

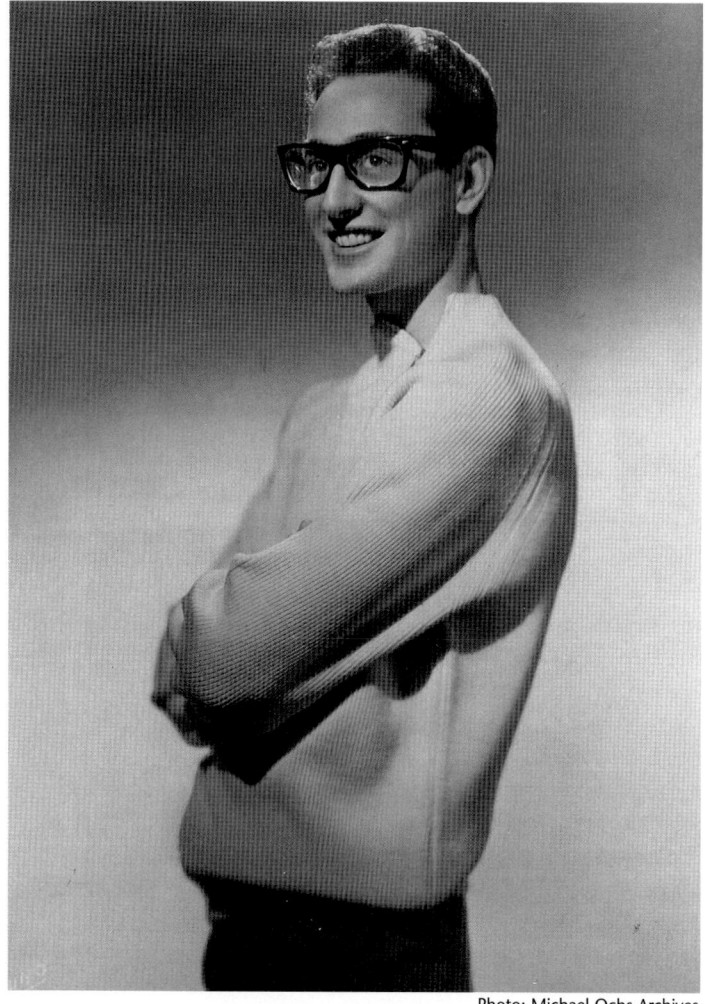

Photo: Michael Ochs Archives

Three

"Everyday, It's A-Gettin' Closer..."
30 Important Dates In Buddy Holly's Life

1. **September 7, 1936**—Charles Hardin Holley is born in Lubbock, Texas.
2. **January 1955**—Buddy meets Elvis Presley at Lubbock's Cotton Club.
3. **October 1955**—In his first major rock 'n' roll gig, Buddy and his singing partner Bob Montgomery open for Bill Haley & His Comets at Lubbock's Fair Park Coliseum.

1956
4. **January 26**—Buddy records his first session in Nashville for Decca Records.
5. **April 16**—Decca issues the first Buddy Holly record, "Blue Days, Black Nights."

Sheet music for "That'll Be The Day," 1957

Photo: Showtime Archives

1957
6. **February 25**—Buddy and his group record the hit version of "That'll Be the Day" in the wee hours, at Norman Petty's recording studio in Clovis, New Mexico.
7. **May 27**—Brunswick Records, a subsidiary of Decca, releases the single of "That'll Be the Day" under the name the Crickets.
8. **June 20**—Coral Records, also a subsidiary of Decca, releases another single, "Words of Love," under Buddy Holly's own name, as a solo artist, thus establishing two simultaneous avenues for his music.
9. **June 30 or July 1**—Buddy and his group record "Peggy Sue" and "Oh, Boy!" during a late-night session in Clovis.
10. **August 16**—The Crickets begin a week of performances at the famed Apollo Theater in Harlem.
11. **September 1**—The Crickets begin the Biggest Show of Stars for 1957, which takes them to 80 cities over the next three months.
12. **September 20**—Coral releases the second Buddy Holly single, "Peggy Sue," which enters *Billboard's* Top 40 three weeks later and peaks at number three.
13. **September 23**—According to *Billboard*, "That'll Be the Day" becomes the top-selling single in the country.
14. **October 27**—Brunswick releases the second Crickets single, "Oh, Boy!," which enters the Top 40 over a month later and tops out at #10.

15. **November 27**—Brunswick Records releases *The Chirpin' Crickets* album, now considered one of the five greatest rock 'n' roll LPs of the 1950s.

16. **December 1**—The Crickets make their national TV debut performing "That'll Be the Day" and "Peggy Sue" on *The Ed Sullivan Show* in New York.

1958

17. **January 26**—The Crickets make their second and final appearance on *The Ed Sullivan Show*, singing only one song, "Oh, Boy!"

18. **January 30**—The Crickets perform in Sydney, Australia, beginning a six-day tour Down Under.

19. **February 12**—Brunswick releases the Crickets' third single, "Maybe Baby," which goes Top 40 a month later and reaches #17 in April.

20. **March 2**—After arriving in London two days earlier, the Crickets kick off a 25-day British tour by making a BBC-TV appearance at the London Palladium.

21. **April 20**—Coral releases Buddy's fourth solo single, "Rave On," which enters the Top 40 for one week in early June, peaking at #37.

22. **May 27**—Brunswick releases "Think It Over," the Crickets' fourth single. It visits the Top 40 in early August, reaching #27.

23. **July 5**—Coral releases Buddy's fifth single, "Early in the Morning," to cover Bobby Darin's original version with the Rinky Dinks. It peaks on the charts at #32 in late August.

24. **August 24**—Buddy marries Maria Elena Santiago in Lubbock.

25. **October 21**—Buddy records his final studio session, in New York, with a full orchestra; it produces his only stereo recordings, including "True Love Ways," "It Doesn't Matter Anymore" and "Raining in My Heart."

26. **October 28**—The Crickets appear on Dick Clark's *American Bandstand*, lip-synching to "It's So Easy."

27. **November 1**—Buddy calls it quits with the Crickets and gives the group name to Jerry Allison and Joe B. Mauldin.

1959

28. **January 5**—Coral releases Buddy's seventh and last single of his lifetime, "It Doesn't Matter Anymore." It will reach #13 a month after his death.

29. **January 23**—Buddy joins the Winter Dance Party tour in Milwaukee.

30. **February 3**—Buddy Holly, along with Ritchie Valens and J. P. Richardson, is killed in the early hours in a plane crash just outside of Clear Lake, Iowa.

1996 Update

Buddy's parents L.O. and Ella Holley, Norman and Vi Petty, Hi-Pockets Duncan, Dick Jacobs, Bob Thiele, Bill Pickering, drummer Carl Bunch and bassist Don Guess are deceased.

Sonny Curtis, Jerry Allison and Joe B. Mauldin live in the Nashville area and continue to tour and occasionally record as the Crickets.

Travis and Larry Holley still live in Lubbock. Maria Elena Holly lives outside of Dallas.

Four

"Listen To Me"
Buddy Holly's Singles And Albums Released During His Lifetime

RELEASED	TITLES	LABEL/NUMBER
1956		
April 16	Blue Days, Black Nights/Love Me	Decca 29854
December 24	Modern Don Juan/You Are My One Desire	Decca 30166
1957		
May 27	That'll Be the Day/ I'm Looking For Someone to Love*	Brunswick 55009
June 20	Words of Love/ Mailman, Bring Me No More Blues	Coral 61852
August 12	That'll Be the Day/ Rock Around With Ollie Vee**	Decca 30434
September 20	Peggy Sue/Everyday	Coral 61885
October 27	Oh, Boy!/Not Fade Away*	Brunswick 55035
November 27	*The Chirpin' Crickets* LP	Brunswick 54038
November 27	*That'll Be the Day* EP	Decca 2575
1958		
January 12	*The Chirpin' Crickets* EP	Brunswick 71036
February 5	I'm Gonna Love You Too/Listen to Me	Coral 61947
February 12	Maybe Baby/Tell Me How*	Brunswick 55053
February 20	*Buddy Holly* LP	Coral 57210
February 20	*The Sound of the Crickets* EP	Brunswick 71038
April 14	*That'll Be the Day* LP	Decca 8707
April 14	*Listen to Me* EP	Coral 81169
April 20	Rave On/Take Your Time	Coral 61985
May 27	Think It Over/Fool's Paradise*	Brunswick 55072
June 23	Girl on My Mind/Ting-a-Ling	Decca 30650
July 5	Early in the Morning/Now We're One	Coral 62006
Late July	Real Wild Child/Oh You Beautiful Doll***	Coral 62017
September 12	It's So Easy/Lonesome Tears*	Brunswick 55094
November 5	Heartbeat/Well All Right	Coral 62051
1959		
January 5	It Doesn't Matter Anymore/ Raining in My Heart	Coral 62074

*Released as by The Crickets; Buddy Holly's name was not on the label.

**Saxophone version, recorded in November 1956. The more popular rockabilly version of "Ollie Vee," recorded in July 1956, was included on Decca's 1958 *That'll Be the Day* album, but not released as a single until 1964.

***Though recorded by the Crickets lineup, drummer Jerry Allison sang lead, while Buddy played guitar and sang background vocals along with the Roses, who were by late '58 the chorus voices on the Crickets records. The single was released under the name Ivan.

This is the English release of the album that popularized the Sunburst Fender Stratocaster.

Fans who bought this Decca LP of Buddy's Nashville material were shocked to hear a very different "That'll Be the Day."

U.S. Coral repackaged *The Chirpin' Crickets* in 1962.

Photos: Showtime Archives

Five
"Yeah, I'm Gonna Make Those Bells Ring"
Buddy Holly's Chart Hits

SINGLES	U.S. POP	U.S. R&B+	U.K.	AUSTRALIA
That'll Be the Day* (1957)	#1	#2	#1	#2
Peggy Sue (1957)	#3	#2	#6	#2
Oh, Boy!* (1957)	#10	#13	#3	#2
Everyday (1957)	—	—	—	#9
Maybe Baby* (1958)	#17	#4	#4	#15
Listen to Me (1958)	—	—	#16	—
I'm Gonna Love You Too (1958)	—	—	—	#38
Rave On (1958)	#37	—	#5	#29
Think It Over* (1958)	#27	—	#11	—
Fool's Paradise* (1958)	#58	—	—	—
Early in the Morning (1958)	#32	—	#17	#22
It's So Easy* (1958)	—	—	—	#8
Real Wild Child*** (1958)	#68	—	—	—
Heartbeat (1958-59)	#82	—	#30	—
Well All Right (1958-59)	—	—	v	#24
It Doesn't Matter Anymore (1959)	#13	—	#1	#1
Raining in My Heart (1959)	#88	—	—	—
Midnight Shift (1959)	—	—	#26	#7
Peggy Sue Got Married (1959)	—	—	#13	—
Heartbeat (reissued, 1960)	—	—	#30	—
True Love Ways (1960)	—	—	#25	—
Learnin' the Game (1960)	—	—	#36	—
What to Do (1961)	—	—	#34	—
Baby I Don't Care/Valley of Tears (1961)	—	—	#12	—
Listen to Me (reissued, 1962)	—	—	#48	—
Reminiscing (1962)	—	—	#17	—
Wait 'Til the Sun Shines, Nellie (1963)	—	—	—	#24
Brown-Eyed Handsome Man (1963)	—	—	#3	#10
Bo Diddley (1963)	—	—	#4	#5
Wishing (1963)	—	—	#10	—
What to Do**** (reissued, 1963)	—	—	#27	—
I'm Gonna Love You Too (reissued, 1964)	—	—	—	#6
You've Got Love** (1964)	—	—	#40	—
Peggy Sue (reissued, 1964)	—	—	—	#34
Love's Made a Fool of You (1964)	—	—	#39	—
Peggy Sue/Rave On (1968)	—	—	#32	—
True Love Ways (reissued, 1988)	—	—	#65	—

*As by The Crickets
**As by Buddy Holly and the Crickets
***As by Ivan. J.I. Allison sang lead, Buddy sang background vocals.
****Backed by the Fireballs; produced by Norman Petty. The 1961 version had different backing recorded in New York under the direction of Jack Hansen.
+Though four of Buddy's records made the R&B charts, he never charted Country.

U.S. chart positions taken from *Billboard*; compiled by Joel Whitburn. British chart positions taken from *New Musical Express* (before 1960) and *Record Retailer*; compiled by Jo & Tim Rice, and *The Guiness Book of British Hit Singles* by Paul Gambaccini & Mike Reed.

ALBUMS

The Buddy Holly Story (1959)	#11 U.S./#2 U.K.++
The Buddy Holly Story, Part 2 (1960)	#7 U.K.
That'll Be the Day (1961)	#5 U.K.
Reminiscing (1963)	#40 U.S./#2 U.K.
Buddy Holly Showcase (1964)	#3 U.K.
Holly in the Hills (1965)	#13 U.K.
Buddy Holly's Greatest Hits (1967)	#9 U.K.
Giant (1969)	#13 U.K.
Greatest Hits (1st reissue, 1971)	#32 U.K
Greatest Hits (2nd reissue, 1975)	#42 U.K.
Buddy Holly Lives: 20 Golden Greats (1978)	#1 U.K./#1 Germany
Greatest Hits (3rd reissue, 1984)	#100 U.K.
True Love Ways (1989)	#8 U.K.
Words of Love (1992)	#1 U.K.

American album listings are confined to the Top 40 only; British albums include those that charted in the Top 100.
++Charted for 181 weeks in the United States and 156 weeks in Great Britain.

Photos: Showtime Archives

Six

"Changing All Those Changes":
The Unreleased Buddy Holly Album of Alternate Takes You Probably Haven't Heard

As of this writing, the authors are awaiting confirmation of the report that all of the alternate takes from Buddy's three 1956 Decca sessions have been found in Nashville; MCA Records executive Andy McKaie says that the company's lawyers are in negotiations with the owner of the tapes.

In the meantime, there are at least two dozen other Buddy Holly tapes and acetates that exist but have yet to be officially released because of lingering differences among the Buddy Holly and Norman Petty estates and MCA Records. The following tracks would make an excellent album of mostly unheard takes whenever the various parties reach an accord.

1. **Peggy Sue** (take 1)—The hit version was take 2. This unreleased recording sounds similar, but Buddy's delivery is flatter and there's a missed beat when he switches from playing rhythm guitar to the lead solo.

2. **Oh, Boy!**—This is the same take as the hit version, but the overdubbed voices of the "Crickets" (actually a group called the Picks) are absent, revealing the full excitement of Buddy's guitar playing.

3. **Rave On** (takes 1 & 2)—The hit version was take 3.

4. **Words of Love**—On the released version Buddy had overdubbed himself, vocally and instrumentally, at least twice. Both the single-track (the initial run-through) and double-tracked tapes exist.

5. **Reminiscing** (alternate take)—R&B saxophone great King Curtis wrote and played on this one.

6. **Crying, Waiting, Hoping** (alternate take)—This is Buddy singing and playing his guitar, alone, in his Greenwich Village apartment in December 1958. Songs #7 and #8 below were recorded at roughly the same time.

7. **That's What They Say** (takes 1 or 3)—Take 2 has been released twice, with different overdubbed backgrounds.

8. **What To Do** (alternate take)—Same details as "That's What They Say."

9. **Don't Come Back Knocking** (two alternate demo takes recorded at Norman Petty's studio).

10. I'm Changing All Those Changes (alternate take from Buddy's second Decca session).

11. Lonesome Tears—Like "Oh, Boy!" this is the original Crickets tape before background vocals were overdubbed.

12. Send Me Some Lovin'—Same as "Lonesome Tears."

13. It's Too Late—Same as "Lonesome Tears."

14. Last Night—Same as "Lonesome Tears."

15. Think It Over (takes 2 or 3)—The released Crickets single was take 3 overdubbed with background vocals. Take 1 exists but is poorly performed and recorded.

16. Fool's Paradise (takes 2 or 3)—The released Crickets single was take 3 overdubbed with background vocals.

17. Moonlight Baby—This is an alternate demo, with lyric changes, of the song released as "Baby, Won't You Come Out Tonight."

18. Not Fade Away (incomplete alternate take)—Despite the absence of the first verse of the song, this rough-edged alternate take, without overdubbing, gives an insight into Buddy's playing.

Thanks to Bill Griggs for his invaluable help in compiling this list.

Seven
"Like A Talent Scout You Want Some Love That's New"
Cover Records & Remakes of Buddy Holly Songs

During Buddy Holly's lifetime, a dozen or so artists covered his records. A "cover" is a record released either to capitalize on the popularity of the original or to overtake it on the charts with better promotion and distribution. Several big companies, such as Mercury and Dot, made many millions of dollars by covering other artists' records on mostly smaller labels. A cover record should not be confused with a remake.

"Words of Love"
1. The Diamonds (Mercury, #76 Pop, 1957)—This professional cover group, hot on the heels of their #2 smash, "Little Darlin'," shoved aside Buddy's debut Coral single and were the first to put a Buddy Holly composition on the charts. Their upbeat cha cha version bears little resemblance to Buddy's moody original, which never charted. According to lead singer Dave Somerville, "We heard the song on a publisher's demo. It may have been Buddy's recording, I don't remember. We would sit down with our arranger, David Carroll, and come up with arrangements. Since 'Little Darlin'' had a Latin beat, we decided let's not disturb the listener too much, so we gave it a similar Latin sound." Not long afterward, the Diamonds toured with the Crickets for several weeks. "Buddy and I became very close," says Somerville, "but to my recollection he never said anything about us covering his song. I don't think the topic ever came up between us. He was such an easygoing guy, he probably wouldn't have said anything even if it bothered him a little."

"That'll Be the Day"
1. The Ravens (Argo, 1957)—This seminal R&B quartet, whose recording career went back to 1946, was a mere shadow of its original incarnation by the time it covered the song on a Chess Records subsidiary label. The lead vocalist was tenor Joe Van Loan, who had joined the Ravens in 1951; the remaining three members had been with the group less than a year. Not only was the Ravens' single a rare instance of a black group covering a white one, but Van Loan tried, rather badly, to imitate Buddy's vocals. **2. Larry Page (Columbia, 1957)**—Billed as the "Teenage Rage," Page covered the song for the British market, but the Crickets' single invaded the country just in time to abort not only Page's dreadful middle-of-the-road rendition, but his nascent recording career as well. **3. Jeff Allen (Verve, 1957)**—The only "verve" on this poor rock 'n' roll imi-

tation was printed on the record label. Allen later covered Joe B. Mauldin's song, "Last Night." from *The Chirpin' Crickets* LP. **4.** Jerry Case (Tops, 1957)—Tops was a cheapo label, sold in department stores, that copied the hits and put four songs on each single, under the slogan "Twice the Music, Half the Cost." Half the talent, too. "Jerry Case" was probably a pseudonym. **5.** The Tunettes (Embassy, 1957)—This was English singer Johnny Worth's group, working as cover artists for a cut-rate label sold only at S.W. Woolworth's department stores—but since every British town had a Woolworth's, Embassy singles sold quite well, though they weren't tabulated for the record charts. Embassy records were priced at two-thirds the cost of regular singles, featured a hit song on both the "A" and "B" sides, and were often done by popular artists moonlighting behind other names. **6.** Vic Corwin (Puccio, 1958)—Like Tops, Puccio was a cut-rate, 4-songs-on-a-single label sold either in five & dime stores or through mail-order.

"Peggy Sue"
1. Jackie Walker (Imperial, 1957)—A nondescript country singer best known for a song called "Big Fat Rib," Walker crossed over to become a nondescript rockabilly artist with this cover record. **2.** Jack Sheldon (Tops, 1957)—Like Jerry Case above, Jack Sheldon may have been a Tops Records pseudonym. **3.** Rusty York (King, 1957)—York's cover version sold well in a few isolated markets and launched his brief recording career, which culminated in a minor hit rockabilly version of Marty Robbins' "Sugaree." **4.** Paul Rich (Embassy, 1958)—Rich was the pseudonym of an anonymous British cover artist recording for Woolworth's in-store cut-rate label. **5.** Vic Corwin (Puccio, 1958) **6.** Artie Malvin & the Zig Zags (Waldorf, 1958)—Yet another sub-standard group recording for a budget label.

"Everyday"
1. Tina Robin (Coral, 1958)—Buddy's own label covered the flipside of "Peggy Sue" for the easy listening adult market.

"Oh, Boy!"
1. Vic Corwin (Puccio, 1958) **2.** Paul Rich (Embassy, 1958)

Since his death, Buddy's songs have been recorded by artists of nearly every stripe. "That'll Be the Day" alone has been redone by more than 100 artists (including a square dance caller, recording for the hoedown crowd). The following is a selected list of remakes:

"Crying, Waiting, Hoping"
1. Dave Mason (1975)—This English folk rocker gave the song a lively Caribbean treatment, *a la* Jimmy Buffett, and introduced it with the opening verse of "Peggy Sue Got Married," which is not surprising, considering that Buddy's first posthumous single on Coral was "Peggy Sue Got Married" backed with "Crying,

Waiting, Hoping." **2.** Wreckless Eric (late '70s)—Buddy's song proved elastic enough even for punk rock. **3.** Marshall Crenshaw (1987)—Portraying Buddy Holly in the film *La Bamba*, Crenshaw recorded the song live (overdubbed with subsequent studio sweetening) for the soundtrack in a style more suited to '80s power pop than '50s rock 'n' roll. **4.** The Beatles (1994)—The Fab Four, with George Harrison on lead vocal, recorded this song for a January 1962 Decca Records audition (with Pete Best on drums) and cut it live (with Ringo on the skins) at least twice for their 1963 BBC radio appearances. The various versions were frequently bootlegged (the most famous being a single of the Decca demo on the Deccagone label), but none was released officially until the 1994 *Beatles Live at the BBC* CD. As lead guitarist, George slavishly followed the laid-back, not-very-hip licks of New York session guitarist Donald Arnone, who had overdubbed Buddy's home tape of the song after his death. **5.** Marty Stuart and Steve Earle (1995)—Despite Earle's opening Delta blues slide guitar solo, which promised the specter of "Buddy Holly Meets Robert Johnson," this version turned out to be an ordinary rehash reminiscent of Marshall Crenshaw's uptempo rock treatment.

"Everyday"

1. Rocky Hart With The Passions (1959)—Yes, this is the same Rocky Hart who later recorded "Someone Stole My Baby While Doing the Twist." Rocky delivered the song, spelled "Every Day" on the label, with Buddy's mannerisms, while the band gave it a harder backbeat and faster tempo. **2.** Norman Petty Trio (1960)— Buddy's Hammond organ-playing producer and song publisher, along with wife Vi Petty on piano and Jack Vaughn on guitar, presented the ballad as polite and polished lounge mood music suitable for tiki rooms. **3.** Bobby Vee (1960)—Bobby Veline, a North Dakota boy who stood in for Buddy in Fargo on the night of the plane crash, was the most successful of the Buddy Holly imitators, but despite the involvement of Norman Petty, this imitation remains a poor one. Bobby recorded nearly the entire Buddy Holly canon on various albums, but "Everyday" was the only Holly song released as a Bobby Vee single. **4.** Joe Dowell (1961)—Dowell was famous at the time for his #1 hit cover version of Elvis Presley's "Wooden Heart," from *G.I. Blues*. Joe recorded "Everyday" for his *Wooden Heart* album, and pounded a wooden stake through it. **5.** Johnny Sea (1964)—Everyday, as it turned out, would get closer to 1966, when Sea recorded his one Top 40 hit, "Day of Decision," a patriotic answer to Barry McGuire's "Eve of Destruction." It was followed by a long night of obscurity that continues to this day. **6.** Tommy Allsup (1965)—The fleet-fingered lead guitarist on several of Buddy's last recordings, including "It's So Easy" and "Heartbeat," took a few licks at

Buddy's songs on yet another Norman Petty-produced tribute LP called *The Buddy Holly Songbook*, backed by members of the Fireballs. **7.** The Tremeloes (1968)—This British quartet was riding high on both the U.S. and U.K. charts at the time with "Here Comes My Baby" and "Silence Is Golden." **8.** Sleepy LaBeef (#73 C&W, 1968)—This ex-rockabilly singer-guitarist scored his first country hit with Buddy's song, croaked in his trademark deep baritone. **9.** Gordon Waller (1969)—Waller was formerly half of the British pop duo Peter & Gordon (see "True Love Ways"). **10.** The Crickets (1970)—Led by Sonny Curtis, the Crickets looked all the way back across the hazy decade of the 1960s to recall the 1957 song as a super-soft rocker. **11.** John Denver (1971)—The Colorado-high folkie, an alumnus of Lubbock's Texas Tech, gave the song an uplifting tenor rendition guaranteed to ring off the sides of the Rockies and make everybody feel better. **12.** Don McLean (#38 U.K., 1973)—After the success of "American Pie," McLean included this track on an album of favorite songs, giving it the urgency of a folk ballad. **13.** The Oak Ridge Boys (#1 C&W, 1984)—Though Buddy Holly started as a country artist, he never made the country charts. At long last, 25 years after his death, one of his songs reached the top of country music. **14.** James Taylor (#61 Pop, 1985)—Despite this ultra-relaxed version's lukewarm chart performance, it has become a staple of easy listening radio in the 1990s. **15.** The Cliff Adams Singers (1993)—This vocal aggregation, known for its many years on BBC-2 radio's *Sing Something Simple* program, was England's version of the Ray Conniff Singers. Their medley of "Everyday" and "Peggy Sue" is saccharine music for the geriatric, glucose-tolerant crowd—which, come to think of it, nowadays includes many of the original "Peggy Sue" fans.

"Heartbeat"

1. The England Sisters (#30 U.K., 1960)—When this single charted in Great Britain on Her Majesty's Victor, Coral "covered" it by reissuing Buddy Holly's 1958 original, which also reached #30 throughout the Realm. **2.** Dave Berry (1966)—Berry was a wispy but successful British soft rocker during the early Beatles era, but this record came at the end of his time on the charts. He also recorded "Maybe Baby" two years later. **3.** Humble Pie (1969)—This British quartet was one of the early so-called supergroups. It included guitarist Peter Frampton (delivering plenty of power chords) and former Small Faces vocalist Steve Marriott (displaying powerful vocal chords). **4.** Showaddywaddy (#7 U.K., 1975)—This English vocal-instrumental group enjoyed several mid-'70s hits in Great Britain, including a remake of Eddie Cochran's "Three Steps to Heaven," which Eddie had recorded with the Crickets at his very last session. **5.** Denny Laine, with Paul & Linda McCartney (1977)—The song was recorded—rather tentatively—for a tribute album called *Holly Days*. Unfortunately, no isolated track of Linda's caterwauling survives *a la* Wings' live "Hey, Jude." **6.** The Knack (1979)—Singer-guitarist Doug Fieger, a Holly fan from Detroit, included the song on his group's multi-million-selling #1 debut album, *Get the Knack*. **7.** Rebecca Hall (#83 C&W, 1985)—Buddy provided this little songbird with her only flirtation on the country charts, then it was back to ordinary life for Becky. **8.** Nick Berry (#2 U.K., 1992)—Berry stars in a top-rated British series on ITV called *Heartbeat*. A 1994 CD called *The Best of Heartbeat* topped the album charts; author Spencer Leigh wrote the booklet notes. **9.** Connie Francis (1996)—The queen of '50s pop joined Sonny Curtis on this lively Mexican-flavored number for her tribute album to Buddy, complete with Danny Davis's Nashville Brass. It's easily the most commercial track Connie's done in 30 years.

"I'm Gonna Love You Too"

1. Adam Faith (1961)—Faith was England's version of Bobby Vee, a pretty-boy crooner who sounded a little like Holly, complete with hiccups and pizzicato strings. **2.** The Hullaballoos (#56 Pop, 1964)—These blond mop-tops were the English Invasion's most ardent Holly imitators, recording four of his songs in all. They were much better rockers than their overall chart failure would indicate. **3.** Terry Jacks (1974)—He had joy, he had fun, he had "Seasons in the Sun" at the top of the American charts, but surprisingly this ex-Poppy Family hippy-dippy knew at least one Buddy Holly song. **4.** Phil Ochs (1974)—Dressed in an Elvis-style gold lamé suit, folk music's dark angel performed the song in a Buddy Holly medley at his controversial 1970 Carnegie Hall concert. The New York folk crowd, an elitist and pretentious bunch, wasn't pleased. **5.** Blondie (1978)—Debbie Harry whined the song as a sassy, punk-edged brush-off—and quite well, too—but Chris Stein backed her with a pointless and unfocused guitar solo characteristic of every hard rock record of the era.

"I'm Lookin' For Someone to Love"

1. Jackie DeShannon (1964)—Before her mid- to-late '60s chart successes, she was a rockabilly singer. This single had a Buddy Holly song on both sides (the B-side was "Oh, Boy!"), which could almost suggest that Jackie's very first record in 1958, called "Buddy," was an early tribute to Holly. **2.** The Stray Cats (late '80s)—Brian Setzer and company proved conclusively that nothing kills a rockabilly record like heavy overdubbing. **3.** Ray Campi & Tony Conn (1996)—These two former Rollin' Rock Records rockabillies kick the song in the ass, with able backing from boogie-woogie pianist Bobby Mizzell (formerly with the Big Bopper's band) and honking sax legend Big Jay McNeely.

"It Doesn't Matter Anymore"

1. Johnny Worth (1959)—Johnny was best known as a British songwriter (Adam Faith's "What Do You Want"), but he covered Buddy's first posthumous hit as a vocalist for Woolworth's cut-rate Embassy label. **2.** Wanda Jackson (1961)—The Queen of Rockabilly countrified the song, stamping it with her Oklahoma twang: "Hit doesn't matter anymower." **3.** Paul Anka (1963)—Anka wrote the song for Buddy, but he waited a respectable period after the plane crash before recording it himself. Now, if he would just stop telling people he barely missed being on that airplane... **4.** Adam Faith (1964)—Faith had already built his British pop career on the original version's distinctive pizzicato string arrangement, so it was about time that he got around to recording the song itself. **5.** Freddie and the Dreamers (1965)—This British group's version might have sold better had it been more rhythmically suited for lead singer Freddie Garrity's wacky dance, the Freddie. **6.** Linda Ronstadt (#47 Pop, 1975)—This was her introduction to Buddy Holly; she would soon record two more hits of his songs. **7.** R. C. Bannon (#33 C&W, 1978)—This Dallas singer hovered on the edge of the country charts for several years, but he couldn't get past the onus of being Mr. Barbara Mandrell. **8.** Danny Gatton, with Rodney Crowell on vocals (1993)—The great rock guitarist from Baltimore included the song on one of his last albums before he took its lyrics to heart and put a gun to his head. **9.** Suzy Boggus (1995)—Though a leading country voice in her own right, Suzy chose to copy Ronstadt's earlier version when she recorded the song for an MCA Buddy Holly tribute CD.

"It's So Easy"

1. The Legends (1963)—This surf band was so legendary, we have no idea who they were. **2.** Jimmy Gilmer (1964)—This Texas singer fronted the Fireballs for 1963's #1 hit and top-selling single, "Sugar Shack," produced by Norman Petty. Gilmer and Petty included "It's So Easy" on a tribute album called *Buddy's Buddy*, even though Jimmy and Buddy never met. **3.** Waylon Jennings (1964)—Buddy's real buddy and bass player roused himself from his post-plane crash funk to record this song at a Phoenix nightclub during an after-hours session. **4.** Skeeter Davis (1967)—The popular country star of the '60s and '70s dedicated an entire album to Buddy, with help from Waylon Jennings and moral support from Buddy's parents, who watched most of the songs being recorded. **5.** Andy Williams (#13 U.K., 1970)—Don't ask. **6.** The Crickets (1970)—It's extremely difficult to go back and do rock 'n' roll as well as you did the first time, when you were much younger, as Holly's former group, featuring Sonny Curtis on vocals, proved convincingly. **7.** Denny Laine, with Paul & Linda McCartney (1977)—By singing a medley of "Listen to Me" and "It's So Easy,"

Laine demonstrated the melodic and structural similarities of the two songs—and why not? Buddy wrote them both at about the same time. McCartney, who produced this material, recorded it at home on a mono tape machine and then processed everything electronically for stereo—a kind of technological joke, perhaps. **8.** Linda Ronstadt (#5 Pop, 1977)—Buddy was Linda's main muse by now.   **9.** Waylon Jennings (1978)—This time Waylon recorded the song with the Crickets as part of a Buddy Holly medley.   **10.** Chris Spedding (1989)—The New York new wave artist merely gave the song a conventional reading.

"Learning the Game"

1. The Searchers (1964)—Hot off the success of their single, "Needles and Pins," this British Invasion beat group recorded the song on a live album under the title "Led in the Game."   **2.** The Hullabaloos (1965)—The blond-mopped British quartet sped up the song and gave it a classic Holly vocal and guitar treatment. If Buddy had ever gotten around to recording "Learning the Game" in the studio, this is what it may have sounded like.   **3.** Sandy Denny & The Bunch (1972)—The cream of Great Britain's folk contingent included Fairport Convention's Richard Thompson and Miss Denny, here proclaiming that unlike their rock 'n' roll-hating American counterparts, they loved Buddy Holly and could do his music passably well.   **4.** Harvey Andrews (1972)—This is the British singer who wrote "Don't Get on the Plane." Rock critics and record buyers shouted back, "Don't go in the studio!"   **5.** Waylon Jennings with Mark Knopfler (1995)—Waylon has said that Buddy had planned to record this song with him, so who's more qualified to record it now?

"Listen to Me"

1. The Searchers (1963)—This popular British group, best known for "Love Potion Number 9," named themselves after the same John Wayne film that gave Buddy the tag line "That'll be the day." Their "Listen to Me" followed Buddy's blueprint, note for note.   **2.** The Hollies (#11 U.K., 1968)—They took his name, so it was about time this English quartet got around to singing one of Buddy's songs.   **3.** Denny Laine, with Paul and Linda McCartney (1977)—See "It's So Easy."

"Love's Made a Fool of You"

1. The Crickets (#26 U.K., 1959)—After Buddy split from the group, one of their next sessions, in December 1958, produced this version of a song that Buddy had only recorded as a demo. The Crickets' lead singer at the time was Earl Sinks. Brunswick released the song three weeks after the plane crash as the sixth Crickets single. Though it sold well in England, the single didn't make the slightest dent on the American charts. Holly's original demo version wasn't released until 1964.   **2.** Sammy Kaye & His Orchestra (1964)—Pardon us while we scratch our heads.

3. Tom Rush (1965)—The first of the American folk singers to publicly declare his love for Buddy, Rush gave the song a tasty, relaxed treatment on wax, and made it a staple at his live shows. **4.** Bobby Fuller Four (1966)—As a follow-up to their big hit, "I Fought the Law," which they'd taken off a 1961 Crickets album, Fuller and company picked this one off the same *In Style With the Crickets* album, with Jim Reese supplying Holly-flavored guitar licks. **5.** Sandy Denny & The Bunch (1972)—Following Tom Rush's blueprint, the Scottish folksinger made this ditty sound like a lilt from the mists of time.

"Maybe Baby"
1. Esquerita (Capitol, 1959)—This R&B veteran, one of Little Richard's inspirations, ripped the song to shreds on his first album for Capitol Records, pounding his piano like a maniac and screaming in a hoarse rasp. **2.** The Derringers (1961)—This Capitol Records pop vocal group might've been white or politely black. We don't know. **3.** Leaping Ferns (1964)—This group was actually the surf band called the Chantays, of "Pipeline" fame. **4.** Jackie DeShannon (1964)—Jackie seemed to have had a thing for Buddy early in her career. **5.** The Serendipity Singers (1966)—This sappy-dippy Colorado folk-pop group gave the song a hootenanny treatment, in (vain) hopes of returning to the Top 40 after their classic "Beans in My Ears." **6.** The Outsiders (1966)—This Cleveland group with a British sound put four hits in the Top 40 that year, including "Time Won't Let Me," but they saved "Maybe Baby" for their album. **7.** Dave Berry (1968)—The single did less than modest business in England, telling Berry that maybe his former chart career as a rocker was truly done with. **8.** Raw (1971)—Raw was a British studio group, featuring singer Ian Campbell and guitarist Zed Jenkins, put together for a Buddy Holly tribute LP called *Raw Holly*. They gave "Maybe Baby" a mild psychedelic treatment, making it the most distinctive track on what is mostly a spotty album. **9.** Gallery (1972)—Jim Gold, the leader of this Detroit sextet, included the song on the album that followed their big hit, "Nice to Be With You." **10.** Susie Allanson (#7 C&W, 1978)—Buddy's song kick-started her country music career, which lasted for a couple of years. **11.** The Nitty Gritty Dirt Band (1995)—By this time most of the nitty gritty, not to mention dirt, had been scrubbed away from this band's music. But wouldn't that describe just about every modern record by any group from the '60s and '70s? On the plus side, when the Nitty Gritty Dirt Band played Lubbock in 1971 and discovered to their chagrin that most of their youthful audience had no idea who Holly was, they played a medley of his songs to enlighten them.

"Not Fade Away"
1. Bobby Fuller (1962)—Fuller was a successful Holly imitator who would

later hit big as the leader of the Bobby Fuller Four with a post-Holly Crickets song called "I Fought the Law." But on this, Bobby's first single, released on the tiny Eastwood label, he overdubbed all the instruments and voices himself in his home studio.   **2.** The Rolling Stones (#48 Pop, #3 U.K., 1964)—This was the group's first American hit (their third in Britain), done the way Bo Diddley might have recorded the song had he thought about it in 1964, when he still had fire in the belly (see below) and a harmonica player like Mick Jagger at his disposal.   **3.** Dick & Deedee (1964)—Dick St. John and DeeDee Sperling (he sang the girl parts, she sang the boy parts—thanks to overdubbing, their performances were always quartets or sextets) were still famous for "The Mountain's High" from three years earlier, but Buddy's song provided a lull in their career.   **4.** Corporate Image (1966)—"Not Fade Away" by Corporate Image—on MGM Records? Is that an oxymoron?   **5.** Joe Pass (1966)—The legendary jazz guitarist gave rock 'n' roll a chance.   **6.** Group Axis (1969)—This hippie group was tied in with the Grateful Dead.   **7.** The Grateful Dead (1971)—Jerry Garcia, Bob Weir and company considered Buddy's song an integral part of their marathon concerts; Mickey Hart tried to take the beat back to its West African patted juba origins with his talking drums.   **8.** The Everly Brothers (1972)—Brothers Don and Phil claim that Buddy originally wrote the song for them.   **9.** Phil Ochs (1974)—Phil's heart was in the right place, but he wasn't a rocker. **10.** Bo Diddley (1978)—Diddley says Buddy ripped him off when he wrote this song, but that didn't stop Bo from recording it as an interminable jam with some very heavy (and heavy handed) session musicians. Bo seems to have forgotten that he borrowed "Bo Diddley" from "Hambone," by the Hambone Kids—the same source from which the Crickets reportedly got "Not Fade Away."   **11.** Tanya Tucker (#70 Pop, 1979)—Her MCA single, sung in a gritty rock 'n' roll voice, announced that she was no longer the little Texas country girl of "Delta Dawn." She even wore black leather to promote the song. But when the flipside, "Texas (When I Die)," rose high into the country charts, while "Not Fade Away" faded fast, Tanya thought that maybe she'd better stick with country.   **12.** The Lolitas (1989)—This New York-based, partly European unisex punk band sounds like Joan Jett with a French or German accent. **13.** The Band with the Crickets (1995)—With Levon Helm singing, The Band, with only minor help from the Crickets, loped through the song with an arrangement that sounds more like the Grateful Dead than the Grateful Dead did.

"Oh, Boy!"

1. Billy & the Glens (1959)—The swirling mists of history have swallowed them up, perhaps never to reveal the true identity of Billy, much less the Glens.   **2.** Jackie DeShannon

(1964)—Before her mid- to-late '60s chart successes, she was a rockabilly singer. This single had a Buddy Holly song on both sides (the A-side was "Looking For Someone to Love"). **3. Johnny Kidd & the Pirates (1964)**—This legendary British rocker, best known for his eyepatch and the original "Shakin' All Over," was considered to be the most credible pre-Beatles rocker. He met his own death in a motorcycle accident not long afterward. **4. Lonnie Mack (1965)**—The guitarist, born Lonnie McIntosh, was still looking for a Top 10 follow-up to "Memphis," without much luck. **5. The Pickering Brothers (a.k.a. The Picks) (1970)**—This was the trio that sang background vocals on Brunswick's original Crickets recording of "Oh, Boy!" **6. Diana Trask (#21 C&W, 1975)**—This Australian-born singer was a regular visitor to the country charts from the late '60s to the early '80s. **7. Mud (#1 U.K., 1975)**—When this group sang the song as a chorus of voices, with minimal instrumentation, they did it almost as a joke, then mysteriously found themselves at the very top of Great Britain's singles charts. **8. Bo Donaldson and the Heywoods (1976)**—Two years earlier, in the aftermath of the Vietnam War, this Cincinnati group had recorded America's #1 song: the anti-war "Billy, Don't Be a Hero." Their schlocky version of Buddy's "Oh, Boy!" was merely anti-rock 'n' roll. **9. Joe Brown (1979)**—Brown was Britain's first home-grown rockabilly guitarist; he backed up Eddie Cochran and Gene Vincent on their 1959-60 tours. The Cockney lad was also a fairly good singer. **10. Wanda Jackson (1986)**—The Queen of Rockabilly recorded the song with a Swedish band. Like too many neo-rockabilly outfits, they used way too much 24-track studio wizardry in a doomed attempt at capturing a primitive sound. **11. Joe Ely (1995)**—He's from Lubbock, but he ain't no Buddy Holly. **12. Billy Connolly**—This is an honorable mention: The Scottish comedian sang a parody of "Oh, Boy!"—"All my life I've been kissin', your left tit 'cause your right one's missing!" Elvis would've called it a one-sided love affair.

"Peggy Sue"
1. Bobby Vinton (1961)—Haven't heard it; don't want to. **2. Bobby Vee & the Crickets (1962)**—Buddy's main imitator linked up with Buddy's group for an album: *Bobby Vee Meets the Crickets*. **3. Tommy Allsup (1965)**—This was probably the best cut on Allsup's otherwise ho-hum *Buddy Holly Songbook* LP. **4. The Tremeloes (1968)**—This British quartet put a couple of easy ballads on the U.S. charts, but "Peggy Sue" was a bit of a stretch for them. **5. Ray Allen & the Upbeats (1969)**—This single was a tribute of sorts; Ritchie Valens' "La Bamba" was the B-side. **6. Sandy Nelson (1968)**—Not many rock 'n' roll drummers had their own hit records ("Teen Beat") and a list of over a dozen albums, but Sandy pulled it off; here he pounded the skins in an echo chamber, accompa-

nied by a tinny organ and rhythm guitar. **7. John Lennon (1975)**—In 1973 Lennon teamed with Phil Spector to make an oldies album, but the project dissolved when Spector disappeared. A year later John decided to complete the album. But first he visited Mick Jagger at Jagger's Long Island summer home, and the two of them packed up their guitars and went sailing. While floating in Long Island Sound, the two played through all the rock 'n' roll classics they could think of, and John wrote many of them down, including "Peggy Sue" and "That'll Be the Day." When he went into a New York studio in October 1974, John laid down nine tracks, including "Peggy Sue," which he cut as a faithful reproduction of Buddy's original, right down to the hiccups in all the right places. The echo-laden song was released by Capitol on the official John Lennon *Rock 'N' Roll* oldies album and by a New York Mafia-connected record shark on a mail-order album called *Roots*. **8. Mike Berry (1976)**—Berry, famous for the 1961 U.K. hit, "Tribute to Buddy Holly," has made a mini-career out of singing Buddy's songs. **9. Jerry Jeff Walker (1977)**—This Texas troubadour, best known for "Mr. Bojangles" and his poignant songs about Texas girls, finally got around to saluting his homeboy... and another Texas girl. **10. The Beach Boys (1980)**—Studio overkill, anyone? **11. The Hollies (1980)**—The group that named themselves after Holly finally got around to producing their own tribute album, including this song, executed and recorded exactly how you'd expect from aging millionaires. **12. Tav Falco's Panther Burns (1989)**—This weird retro-'50s guy, with help from guitarist Alex Chilton (formerly of the Box Tops), lisps and waves his hands and perhaps even dances around the microphone during his performance, spoofing in fey and funny form all the girlish cooing that Buddy gave the original. **13. The Cliff Adams Singers (1993)**—This vocal aggregation, known for its many years on BBC-2 radio's *Sing Something Simple* show, was England's version of the Ray Conniff Singers. Their medley of "Peggy Sue" and "Everyday" sounds like Mitch Miller might've been doing the directing. **14. Connie Francis (1996)**—Sonny Curtis rewrote the words for her, making the song a convoluted complaint about how Peggy Sue was taking away Connie's boyfriend.

"Peggy Sue Got Married"

1. Rikki Henderson (1959)—Henderson was a pseudonym of an unknown male singer recording for Woolworth's Embassy label in the United Kingdom. **2. The Crickets (1960)**—Holly's former group gave the song the classic "Peggy Sue" rhythm. Lead singer David Box, a Holly sound-alike from Lubbock, died in his own plane crash four years later. **3. Dave Mason (1975)**—See "Crying, Waiting, Hoping." **4. The Reggaebilly Ripcats (1995)**—Belizean immigrant Shehene Bedran and his Los Angeles band, with R&B legend

Big Jay McNeely on tenor sax, recorded the song with a frantic reggae rhythm, combined with classic Holly guitar work. The recording was produced by Jim Dawson. 5. Buddy Holly & the Hollies (1995)—At last, Buddy's namesakes got the chance to record with him, thanks to modern technology that allowed engineers to alter Buddy's original 1959 tape and credibly overdub it with the Hollies.

"Rave On"
1. Sonny West (1958)—West wrote and recorded the song first (for Atlantic Records), but Buddy's was the hit version and the only one people remember, so for our purposes we'll call "Rave On" a Buddy Holly song, okay? 2. Waylon Jennings (1963) 3. The Outlaws (1964)—This was not Waylon's later group, the Outlaws, nor Mike Berry's group that earlier recorded "Tribute to Buddy Holly." 4. Steeleye Span (1971)—This acappella rendition remains the ultimate remake of a Buddy Holly song—bizarre and yet very listenable. 5. The Nitty Gritty Dirt Band (1972) 6. Denny Laine, with Paul & Linda McCartney (1976)—Another near acappella version, but including Linda McCartney, whose voice wasn't meant to be heard with only minimal audio distraction. 7. Marshall Crenshaw (1983)—With just his voice and acoustic guitar, Crenshaw caught Buddy Holly's spirit perfectly. Released on a Warner Brothers promo EP only, this version is hard to find but worth the search. 8. Jerry Naylor (#80 C&W, 1978)—This so-so ex-Cricket (from the group's early '60s period) managed to keep his so-so country music career going for a couple of years. 9. Rick Nelson (1986)—During his last years Rick sang this song often and recorded it at one of his final sessions. "Rave On" was also his encore song at his last concert, hours before his death. His farewell words to the audience were, "Rave on for me!"

"Stay Close to Me"
1. Lou Giordano (1959)—Though Buddy wrote this song, he never recorded it. Instead, he and Phil Everly produced this single for Brunswick Records. The fact that Giordano sounded like a wimpy version of Holly's friend, Paul Anka, did not bode well for Buddy's nascent production career. All right, we've stretched the meaning of a remake record, but we just had to include this song. 2. Mike Berry (1979)—The British artist best known for "Tribute to Buddy Holly" recorded the song the way he thought Buddy would have done it, if Buddy had too much time and too many tracks in the studio.

"Take Your Time"
1. Carolyn Hester (1958)—Though later known as a Greenwich Village-based folk singer who gave Bob Dylan his start, Hester recorded her first session with Norman Petty—accompanied by Buddy Holly on guitar. 2. Peter & Gordon (1964)

"That'll Be the Day"
1. Fanfare (1959)—If you've got the

record, send us a tape. **2.** Pat Boone (1961)—Pat imbued the song with the same fire and grit he gave "Tutti Frutti," and he never even scuffed his white bucks. **3.** J. Frank Wilson & the Cavaliers (1964)—Wilson, a Texan, was hot off the success of a #1 teen death record called "Last Kiss." **4.** The Everly Brothers (#30 U.K., 1965)—Don and Phil changed the tempo around, turning the song into a march. **5.** The Crossfires (1965)—This California surf band later evolved into the Turtles. **6.** The Statler Brothers (#37 C&W, 1966)—This Virginia quartet was still looking for a hit follow-up to their first big smash, "Flowers on the Wall," earlier in the year. **7.** Francoise Hardy (1968)—The sultry French star gave the song a sexy treatment. Who cares if you can't understand the words very well? **8.** Tommy Roe (1968)—Roe began his career as a Buddy Holly imitator whose first hit record, "Sheila," in 1962, was a take-off on "Peggy Sue." **9.** The Crickets (1970)—With drummer Jerry Allison singing lead, the Crickets sounded much older and mellower than their first time around. **10.** Kenny Vernon (#56 C&W, 1972) **11.** Foghat (1973)—Ham-handed British boogie and blues rock, anyone? **12.** Linda Ronstadt (#11 pop, 1976)—Even with a guitarist burdening her with confused and pointless instrumentation, Linda managed to put Buddy's song back on the charts. **13.** Pure Prairie League (#98 C&W, 1976)—This Cincinnati country band would later launch the career of singer-guitarist Vince Gill. **14.** Link Wray (1982)—This classic power-chord guitarist, best known for "Rumble" back in '58, gave the song a relatively conventional reading while doodling in his home studio. **15.** Bobby Vee (1990)—Vee recorded this version in 1960 with his original group, the Shadows, at Norman Petty's studio, backed with the vocal group the Roses, who had also sung on two Holly singles. It was held back from release on his *I Remember Buddy Holly* album and his weaker 1963 remake with Los Angeles studio musicians was used instead. **16.** The Beatles (1995)—Though not commercially released until 25 years after their breakup, this was the very first recording by John Lennon (singing lead), Paul McCartney, George Harrison and pianist John "Duff" Lowe, captured in 1958 on a Liverpool Art College tape recorder and transferred to shellac at a Liverpool studio, possibly Welsby Sound Recordings. At the time, they were calling themselves the Quarry Men. Two decades later, when the disc had been forgotten, Lowe announced that he was putting it up for auction. Turning down Paul McCartney's offer of $10,000, Lowe hoped to sell it for twice that much on the open market, but he was eventually forced by the British High Court to turn the record over to McCartney, who was the owner of the copyright for "That'll Be the Day" in 1981.

"True Love Ways"

1. Vi Petty (1960)—Norman Petty's wife was the first to record a demo of this song, in the summer of 1958, even before Buddy got around to doing it. In fact, though Buddy wrote the music (based on his favorite gospel song, "I'll Be Alright," by the Angelic Gospel Singers), he had to learn Norman Petty's lyrics from Vi's recording, which was subsequently pressed up on Petty's private label, NorVaJak, as a giveaway to friends, fans and a few disc jockeys over a year after Buddy's death. Coral released a single of Buddy's version several months later. **2. Jimmy Gilmer (1960)**—After both Buddy Holly and the Crickets moved on, Norman Petty made this young Texas singer his next protégé and teamed him with an instrumental group called the Fireballs. The flipside of the single, released on Warwick, was another Holly co-composition, "Wishing," whose original version by Buddy himself wouldn't be released for a couple more years. Gilmer's two tracks here would later be part of a 1964 Petty-produced tribute album called *Buddy's Buddy*; but Gilmer is best remembered for his #1 hit, "Sugar Shack," 1963's biggest selling single. **3. Frank Ifield (1964)**—Australian-born and British-bred, Ifield is best known for parodying Slim Whitman's falsetto yodeling on his 1962 hit version of "I Remember You." **4. Peter and Gordon (#14 Pop, #2 U.K., 1965)**—Britishers Peter Asher and Gordon Waller had good luck on both sides of the Atlantic with this lush arrangement. **5. The Crickets (1970)**—Sonny Curtis assumed lead vocal duties on this ultra-smooth rendition for an album salute to Buddy. **6. Randy Gurley (#78 C&W, 1978)**—Whatever happened to Randy Gurley? **7. Mickey Gilley (#1 C&W, #66 Pop, 1980)**—Gilley, owner of Gilley's, the Pasadena, Texas, club where *Urban Cowboy* was filmed, was riding the crest of his popularity when this single followed in the wake of the movie's phenomenal success. **8. Cliff Richard (#8 U.K., 1983)**—Though practically unknown in America, Richard was probably Great Britain's biggest rock act before the Beatles; even after the music scene changed in 1963, he continued to dominate the charts as a pop act. **9. Rick Nelson (1986)**—At one of his last sessions, Rick turned the song into a poignant, minor-key folk number. **10. The Mavericks (1995)**—This rock-flavored country band has been wowing critics and fans alike; wouldn't know it from this recording, though.

"Well All Right"

1. Russ Vestee (1961)—The flipside of this Amy Records single was a remake of Lee Andrews & the Hearts' "Teardrops," which Vestee also did badly. **2. Bobby Vee & the Crickets (1962)**—Well all right. **3. Bobby Sherman (1965)**—You're asking yourself, whatever happened to '60s teen fave Bobby Sherman? Could this recording be a clue? **4. Blind Faith (1969)**—Stevie Windwood and Eric Clapton, fronting this early supergroup, put Buddy's song into an interesting minor key. **5.** Nanci Griffith with the Crickets (1995)—Griffith, known for her personal songs, doesn't seem to connect with this one, and the Crickets are no help either.

"Wishing"

1. Jimmy Gilmer (1960)—See "True Love Ways" above. This cut was originally issued on Warwick. After its inclusion on a 1964 Buddy Holly tribute LP, it was reissued on Dot Records with a non-Holly song on the flipside. **2.** The King Bees (1980)—Following the blueprint of the '58 Crickets, Jamie James—with his Stratocaster slung low—led this Los Angeles power pop-rockabilly trio, which also recorded the Clovers' 1952 R&B hit, "Ting-a-Ling," exactly the way Buddy Holly cut it for Decca in '56. **3.** Bobby Vee (1992)—Vee made this recording with his own group, the Shadows, in early 1960 at Norman Petty Studios, backed by Vi Petty on piano and the Roses on background vocals, but it stayed in the can for over 30 years. So did a second, less impressive version he made a year later with Ernie Freeman in Los Angeles. **4.** Mary Chapin Carpenter and Kevin Montgomery (1995)—One of today's top country stars teamed up with the son of Bob Montgomery, Holly's early singing and songwriting partner, to give Buddy & Bob's ballad a sweet Nashville treatment worthy of the country charts.

"Words of Love"

1. The Beatles (1965)—With John and Paul harmonizing on the lead vocals, the Fabsters reproduced the song almost chord for chord for their fourth LP, *Beatles For Sale* (released in the U.S., with two less songs, as *Beatles VI*)—at a time when every Beatles album sold millions and dominated rock radio. The group had already recorded "Words of Love" a couple of times earlier during their 1963 BBC radio appearances. On a much later compilation LP of Beatles love songs, this would be the only inclusion from a songwriter outside of the group—but of course Paul McCartney does own the publishing. **2.** Super Mazebe (1983)—The song here is called "Malaba D'Amour," sung in French by this African vocal group, on Virgin Records, performed uptempo with a bright juju-style guitar and a horn section. **3.** The Shoes (1989)—This rock trio gave the song a lush treatment with heavy overdubbing and an almost hypnotic repetition of the song's melodic main guitar hook. **4.** Jim Dawson also remembers hearing an excellent Jamaican reggae version of "Words of Love," retitled "Love Is Real," but has been unable to track it down.

Trade advertisement, 1964
Photo: Jim Dawson

Eight
"Your Love For Me Has Got To Be Real"
Paeans, Dirges and Tribute Records

Though now rare, tribute records to fallen musical heroes go back to the death of country star Jimmie Rodgers in 1933—and probably before that. They generally range from the maudlin and mournful to the bizarre, but they do constitute a genre unto themselves. Buddy Holly has inspired more than his share of them.

1. "Three Stars" by Tommy Dee with Carol Kay & the Teen-Aires—This treacly eulogy on Crest Records was written by Tommy Donaldson, a San Bernardino disc jockey, on the day of the crash. After he announced the tragic news on the air, Donaldson was astonished by the rush of emotional, often sobbing phone calls that came into the station from young fans, so as he was driving home from his shift, Donaldson began jotting down lyrics whenever the rush-hour traffic came to a standstill. The song was meant to be recorded by Eddie Cochran (see #3 below), but when Eddie became too overwhelmed by the lyrics, Donaldson recorded it himself under his nom de jock, Tommy Dee. A month later "Three Stars" began filling the nation's airwaves with religious hokum. "Look up in the sky, up toward the north, There are three new stars, brightly shining forth... Gee, we're gonna miss you, everybody sends their love." Holly is introduced in the middle of the song, between Ritchie Valens and the Big Bopper. "On the right stands Buddy Holly, with a shy grin on his face, Funny how you'd always seem to notice that one little curl out of place... Buddy's singing for God now, in his chorus in the sky, Buddy Holly, we'll always remember you with tears in our eyes." Dee later admitted, "A lot of people thought I had a feel for Buddy Holly on the record, which was strange, because I had never met him. I felt, just from looking at his picture, that he was a shy and bashful type of guy." *Billboard* pronounced "Three Stars" a "Sincere offering that merits airplay." Shamelessly maudlin, "Three Stars" charted in the Top 40 from mid-April into June and reached as high as #11—proof that America in 1959 was a kinder, gentler, more naive place than today. Carol Kay, featured prominently in the song's chorus, is rumored to be Annette Kleinbard, lead singer of the Teddy Bears of "To Know Him, Is to Love Him" fame.

2. "Three Stars" by Ruby Wright, with Dick Pike—King Records' substandard cover disc of Tommy Dee's record took advantage of the song's religious imagery by adding a funereal organ. *Billboard* on March 23, 1959, described it as "Dual track warble on

a pretty waltz." Although Cincinnati disc jockey Dick Pike spoke Dee's recitation (rather mechanically) and Wright sang Carol Kay's secondary chorus (also mechanically), it was she who got top billing on the label. Ruby also garbled Dee's "Look up in the sky, up toward the north" as "Look up in the sky, up to one who knows." The record received no U.S. action beyond Cincinnati, but when Parlophone released it in Great Britain over the summer, the song rose to #19 on the *New Musical Express* chart.

3. "Three Stars" by Eddie Cochran. This was the original demo recording of Tommy Donaldson's song, cut at Gold Star in Hollywood on the night of February 5, 1959, only three days after the crash, for American Music Publishing. Accompanying himself with only a guitar, Cochran recorded the most intriguing and emotional rendition. A catch in his voice betrayed his close friendship with Holly and Valens. But it was precisely this choked-up reading that convinced Tommy Donaldson that he should record the song himself, under his on-air name Tommy Dee. (Crest Records, which released Dee's version, was American Music's in-house demo label.) Eddie's version, cobbled together from several different takes, was to have been released later as a charity single for the families of the dead artists, but his record company, Liberty Records, decided not to put it out—and the cut never saw daylight until it was released in Great Britain in 1966. Cochran avoided small airplanes after the plane crash because he feared for his own safety, but it didn't work; an auto accident near London killed him in 1960.

4. "The Ballad of Donna and Peggy Sue (A Tribute to Ritchie Valens and Buddy Holly)" by Ray Campi—This song was recorded a day or so after Eddie Cochran's "Three Stars," but it was almost certainly the first tribute to the three fallen singers to be released—on February 9, 1959, less than a week after the crash. Campi, an Austin rockabilly singer who'd recorded briefly for Norman Petty in 1958, wrote the song with Austin deejay Jerry Green immediately after hearing the news. He recorded it for the Big Bopper's former label, D Records, at the Starday studio in Houston, backed by the Big Bopper's studio band, including saxophonist Link Davis and guitarist Hal Harris. Campi sings lugubriously, in the style of Ritchie Valens' "Donna," to the lonely ladies in the title: "I knew a girl whose love was more than true, She loved a boy who called her Peggy Sue." Ray assumes the personas of both departed singers to counsel Donna and Peggy, "Don't be lonely, don't be blue," because "I'll never be apart from you… I'm just a thought away." The highlight is the bridge, which Campi sings uptempo in a Hollyesque vocal. The flipside was "The Man I Met (A Tribute to the Big Bopper)."

5. "Three Young Men" by Lee Davis. Old West songs were still popular in May 1959, when this tribute rode onto the stage, so Davis laid on the cowboy imagery pretty heavily: "Three young men took an airplane ride, out to tour the countryside, Three young men out of the West, Now we lay them down to rest... Three young girls are crying tears... How they begged them not to go." It almost sounds like Buddy, Ritchie and the Bopper died in a gunfight. Naturally the whole business is enveloped by a heavily echoed vocal chorus straight out of a Hollywood Western.

6. "The Great Tragedy" by Herschel Almond & the Al Good Band. In March of '59, Mississippi-based Ace Records contributed this doleful opus written and recorded by a Louisiana disc jockey. Today the single is better known for its rockabilly flipside, "Let's Get It On." This seems to have been Almond's only venture into the recording studio. "The Great Tragedy" features a skating rink organ and a corny male chorus that echoes the last words of each phrase. The names of the three stars aren't given, but Almond tells us, "People all came from miles around, just to hear them sing." Later, after "a very special show, together they rode a plane, the rest I'm sure you know." The organ ends the song in a big flourish, not unlike what was then common on soap operas.

7. "Gold Records in the Snow" by Bennie Barnes. This honky tonk number was written and produced by the Big Bopper's close friend, disc jockey George Baxter, and released in late February of '59 as a B-side on D Records (which had released "The Ballad of Donna and Peggy Sue" three weeks earlier). Barnes was himself a Texan from Beaumont, the Big Bopper's home town; he was a Hank Snow-style nasal crooner who three years earlier had enjoyed a big C&W hit with "Poor Man's Riches." His type of country music was miles away from rock 'n' roll, but at least it provided the crash with plenty of hillbilly melodrama: "Buddy Holly, Ritchie Valens, and the biggest Bopper... left 'em rockin' and rollin' in the aisles, then rode into the blue. In the cold dark skies flew a tiny plane—the pilot just left his bride—in the heavens never to return, with three new stars inside. On a lonely farm in Io-way, beside an old fence row, they searched the wreckage just to find, gold records in the snow."

8. "Buddy, Big Bopper, and Ritchie" by Loretta Thompson. This 1960 Skoop Records recitation over an instrumental and choral track was interesting because Loretta expressed her sorrow purely as a fan of their music. "In a small airplane they left an airfield in Iowa, They were never to arrive in Fargo, a show to play... Three young men from far and wide went crashing in the snow... Gee, fellas, why only a few days ago you

were all right here in our town with your big rock 'n' roll show." She treasures the moment she went backstage to get Buddy's autograph and heard him playing his guitar. "You won't be coming back, you won't be making any more records," she laments, but "God must have willed it." In any event, the three rockers will always be in her heart. We don't want to say Miss Thompson lacked talent, but the flipside of her only record was an instrumental.

9. "Tribute to Buddy Holly" by Mike Berry with the Outlaws. Producer Joe Meek, a student of the occult, claimed that he contacted Buddy during a seance to get his permission to record this song by writer Geoff Goddard. (Meek also claimed that during an early 1958 seance he had been told that Buddy Holly would die on February 3, 1958.) Released on the HMV label (Britain's RCA) and banned by the BBC for being in poor taste, the moody "Tribute to Buddy Holly" crested at #24 on the U.K. charts in late 1961, with such lyrics as "The snow was snowin', the wind was a-blowin', when the world said, 'Goodbye, Buddy.'" A preacher could just as easily have included in a Sunday sermon the part of the song that goes, "But still I know that up in heaven, is where we'll see his face again." Mike Berry can still be booked to perform a Buddy Holly tribute set; as for Meek, he murdered his landlady and committed suicide on February 3, 1967—the eighth anniversary of Buddy's death.

10. "Tribute to Buddy Holly" by the Beat Buddies. This 1962 German remake on the Hansa label followed Berry's blueprint, but with better harmonies, a slower tempo and a whistling accompaniment.

11. "Tribute to Buddy Holly" by Chad Allen & the Reflections (later the Guess Who). Not much is known about this record, released on the CA label around 1962, but apparently it did well in Canada.

12. "Tribute to Buddy Holly" by Hep Stars. This Swedish group covered the song for the Scandinavian market on Olga Records (circa 1962). A reliable rumor has it that one of Hep Stars' members was Benny Andersson, who later formed the Swedish pop supergroup ABBA, and that ABBA's second male vocalist, Bjorn Ulvaeus, was one of Hep Stars' songwriters. Hep Stars reformed in the 1980s without Andersson.

13. "Oh Buddy Holly"/"Goodbye and Thanks, Buddy Holly" by the Pilot. In 1961 this Dutch or German group provided solid instrumentals (with what sounds like a Hawaiian guitar) and vocals that generally avoid mimicking Holly's. Both sides are chants, really—"Oh Buddy Holly, oh Buddy Holly... "—as if the members of Pilot were praying to their god: "We all like a star called Buddy Holly, we all play his records twice a day, We don't want another, we love him like a brother, we won't let his music fade away—Oh, Buddy Holly," et al.

14. "Buddy's Song" by Bobby Vee. Vee tried hard to emulate the Holly sound, so much so that he recorded a 1963 album called *I Remember Buddy Holly*. Capping off the album was this number, weaving ten of his song titles—"Blue blue days, long black nights, lonesome tears I tried to cry for you, maybe baby you better start babying me"—into the lyric and mostly taking its melody from Buddy's "Peggy Sue Got Married." The song was purportedly written by Buddy's mother, Ella Holley, but in fact it was composed by Buddy's friend and sideman, Waylon Jennings. There is no mention of the plane crash or of Buddy's death, so perhaps this song doesn't really belong on this list. Fleetwood Mac later recorded it for their 1970 *Kiln House* LP.

15. "The Stage" by Waylon Jennings. Written and recorded by Jennings around 1960-61 when he was still in his mourning period, this narration spoken over a funeral-march drum and a heavenly female chorus, recalls a vision of seeing Holly, Valens, the Big Bopper and Eddie Cochran in what he calls "the greatest show of all." After the others have sung their hits, says Waylon, "The crowd is finally settled back, they know it's time now for the final act. There stands Buddy Holly, smiling, standing tall. His voice is clear, his guitar rings, the angels stand in silence as Buddy sings." The single wasn't released until he signed with Trend Records in 1963. Like Cochran on "Three Stars," Waylon had a hard time getting through the recitation without breaking down; he said later that the only way he could record it was to partition himself off from the other musicians in the studio. When mastering the single, Trend sped up the tape to make Waylon sound younger. Jennings refused to fly in an airplane until 1964.

16. "American Pie—Parts I and II" by Don McLean. It took a dozen years, but finally a tribute to Buddy reached #1 on the U.S. charts and #2 in England, in 1971. Actually this two-sided, eight-and-a-half-minute single on United Artists Records chronicled in mostly obscure metaphors the history of rock 'n' roll up to that point, but it began with "bad news on the doorstep" on "the day the music died," when McLean drove his Chevy to the levy, where "those good ol' boys were drinkin' whiskey and rye, singing 'This'll be the day that I die.'" The amazing success of the song provoked the first Buddy Holly revival in America; Great Britain needed no such thing, because Buddy's records had been charting throughout the '60s.

17. "Buddy Holly Tribute" by Mickey Dolenz. By 1974 Mickey's group, the Monkees, was long dead and Mickey was up a tree, recording for the forgotten Romar label. Though the title of this single suggests a tribute, it was actually a medley of several of Buddy's songs, which is a tribute of

sorts. So why aren't we including other medleys by Buddy Knox, Phil Ochs and Waylon Jennings?

18. "My Buddy Holly Days" by the Rubettes. This 1975 single is one of the most charming Holly tributes. The European group, with a male lead and female chorus, mumbles and harmonizes over a wonderful Hollyesque guitar, explaining how Buddy "left us with his songs of love." At one point they even vie with Peggy Sue for his affections: "Uh-uh-oh, Peggy, do you recall-all, how Buddy fell for you, 'cause we did, yeah we did." The lead singer tosses in all the Holly hiccups and mannerisms.

19. "Old Friend" by Waylon Jennings (1976). Jennings refused for many years to talk about his old friend Buddy Holly, but on this RCA single he recalls their times together, describing how the media represented Buddy. "Old friend, we sure miss you, but you haven't missed a thing."

20. "Tribute to Buddy Holly" by Mike Berry. Berry's more polished 1976 remake of his own 1961 hit became a number-one seller in Belgium and Holland.

21. "Gone Too Soon" by Chuck Travis. On the tiny Energy label, another Holly imitator adds his condolences, lamenting that the music on the radio will never be the same. "This is why I feel so sad and blue-oo, ahoo-hoo, They don't write them like they used to do-oo, ahoo-hoo. Goodbye, Buddy. Goodbye, Ritchie...."

22. "Oh! Buddy (The Music Will Never Die)" by Matlock. Texas singer-keyboardist Stueart Matlock was a Buddy Holly imitator in 1978, but just as so many Elvis impersonators base their acts on the King's Vegas period, Matlock on this single seemed to favor the sound of Holly's New York home tapes, which were overdubbed after his death by a male chorus and uninspired session musicians. The song, on Major Bill Smith's Fort Worth-based LeCam label (better known for recording J. Frank Wilson and Bruce Channel), moves right along: "A lot of good music being played today, but there's one man I really miss, He came by way of Lubbock, Texas, and left his string full of hits." Mindful of Buddy's influence, Matlock wraps it up with "Linda Ronstadt remembered, the Beatles sang 'Words of Love,' the Rolling Stones came with 'Not Fade Away,' all in the memory of..."

23. "Where Are You... Sweet Peggy Sue" by Matlock. This cut off his 1978 album doesn't mention Buddy by name, but rather professes his yearning for Buddy's "girl": "She became a legend, but her story was left untold, and the singer died who turned her name to gold... I just can't forget her, no matter how I try, Maybe I'll meet her by and by." The song may hold the record for most hiccups.

24. "The Real Buddy Holly Story" by Sonny Curtis (1979). Curtis, who played on some of Buddy's first records and later replaced him in the Crickets, was so disappointed by the 1978 film of Buddy's life that he wrote this song to set things right. After recounting their early times together swigging bootleg beer and playing "hot licks in the sun," Curtis laments that "'That'll Be the Day' came much too soon for Buddy." The best line: "Buddy Holly lives every time we sing rock 'n' roll." The record became a minor country hit on Elektra in early 1980.

25. "The Story of Buddy Holly" (1979) by the Familee. "1959 was such a bad year, a great loss for rock 'n' roll," the song begins, as this presumably Dutch group, fronted by a male with an answering female chorus, chants that "20 years later we're singing your songs, they never lost their power and soul." The lead singer, a Holly imitator, hiccups his way through a medley of a dozen of Buddy's songs in this lively tribute, including "Words of Love" which, as the girls in the chorus point out, was later recorded by the Beatles.

26. "I Named My Little Girl Holly" by Buddy Knox. Knox and Holly were Texas boys who began their careers at Norman Petty's studio. Though they shared the same roots, Knox lacked Holly's charisma. This 1980 release was written by a small-time singer named Lee Jackson whose sadness over Buddy Holly's death prompted him to name a daughter after his favorite singer. "There wasn't much else I could do, to best try and remember you, I guess I could have called her Peggy Sue." The song has a nice melody, but Knox's delivery is embarrassingly mawkish, with plenty of "gollys."

27. "I Named My Little Girl Holly" by Mike Berry. This 1980 U.K. edition is less mawkish and more rockish than Buddy Knox's version.

28. "Buddy Holly and the Crickets" by Larry Holley. Released in 1980 on a self-produced album featuring both of Buddy's brothers, a niece, and a nephew, this performance proved once and for all that the Holley family spawned only one musical talent of note.

29. "Buddy Holly Not Fade Away" by the Picks. In this 1980 sequel to Sonny Curtis's "The Real Buddy Holly Story," the Picks—John and Bill Pickering and Bob Lapham, the trio that provided the choral voices of the Crickets on "Oh, Boy!" and "Maybe Baby"—salute Holly's rise from humble beginnings in a country song reminiscent of a Marty Robbins ballad: "Little Buddy Holly was born in '36, Mom and Daddy wasn't poor, but you couldn't call him rich... And he sang his way from a country boy to a place among the stars." Don't worry about Buddy, they sing, because "Mama raised him in the church, and Buddy is at home with God."

30. "The Lubbock Tornado" by Terry Allen. Lubbock singer Allen linked Buddy to a common West Texas force of nature in this 1980 single on the Fate label. "Well, it came in from the southwest, in the middle of the night. Hey, loomed over Lubbock, what a god almighty sight. Yeah, some say it was the ghost of Buddy, others said the ghost of Cain..."

31. "I Feel Like Buddy Holly" by Alvin Stardust. Stardust, a major British rock star in the '70s, was probably feeling like his career had crashed like Buddy's plane when he cut this song by writer Mike Batt in 1984. He said he felt like Buddy "'cause it's raining in my heart." Rather tenuous, wouldn't you say?

32. "Do You Remember Buddy Holly" by Alvis West. This California singer, recording in 1985, complains over a driving beat that today's music is lousy, so he wants to take us back to when rock 'n' roll was pure. "Well, if you remember Buddy Holly, this song's for you," he sings. "Hearing those songs makes me glad, the music and words aren't a fad, they're coming through still for you and me."

33. "A Country Boy (Who Rolled the Rock Away)" by David Allan Coe. This Akron, Ohio-born country star's 1986 Columbia recording was a hosanna to the trinity of Buddy Holly, Hank Williams and Elvis. Coe forgot, however, to include Jesus Christ, another country boy who rolled the rock away. No matter, the single charted anyway—#44 country.

34. "I Won't Forget My Peggy Sue" by Marc Bellin. Bellin, recording for Brownwood Records, was a Nashville country singer who paid Holly a tribute without naming him, in 1987. Backed by a driving country band, he sings, "West Texas roads are the longest, you played me some of the strongest songs I ever heard, I followed you down the line. Now that I think it over, you were ahead of our time." If anyone missed Holly's hidden song titles, the chorus removed all doubt: "Heartbeat, so sweet, ravin' on about you, true love ways, that'll be the day, I forget my Peggy Sue."

35. "Please Don't Get on the Plane" by Harvey Andrews. After writing tributes to Phil Ochs and Harry Chapin, among others, Andrews in 1988 looked back to his days as a 15-year-old Buddy Holly fan in Birmingham, England: "I know that you're tired, and you hired it to go on ahead of the gang, but please don't get on the plane, Take your time like the words of the song you just sang."

36. "Hey Buddy" by Imitation Life. This hard-driving new wave rock song was the opening track on a 1989 album, *Everyday's a Holly Day*, on the Emergo label, of Buddy Holly songs as recorded by young bands few people ever heard of. Lead singer Alan Berman garbles most of the lyrics, so whatever sense they have is generally lost in the grind of guitars.

"You never were too much for shouting, you never raised your voice in pain... will we ever see the likes of you again?"

37. "Buddy's Waiting on the Flatland Road" by Terry Clarke. This British country singer was recording an album in Texas in 1990 when the songs ran out before the tape did. "I looked west out of the window at a brilliant Texas morning and thought of Buddy Holly," he said later. Key line: "He died young so he can't grow old."

38. "Lubbock Calling" by Terry Clarke. Clarke wrote and recorded this tribute in 1990 after seeing Lubbock singer Joe Ely perform. It includes a snatch of "Oh, Boy!" and the key line is: "The ghosts have got it right, Buddy Holly's singing to Joe Ely tonight."

39. "Tribute to Buddy" by Stanley Accrington. Humor seeped into the proceedings for a change when this stalwart of U.K. folk clubs sang in 1991: "He taught me how to be modest, with a talent oh so big, but most of all he taught me, don't catch a plane home after a gig."

40. "Lookin' For the Hi-D-Ho" by Tinker Carlin. In 1991, Carlin, an old acquaintance of Buddy's, wrote and recorded this affectionate song about Lubbock's most popular 1950s drive-in restaurant; Larry Holley produced it for his own "Cloud 9" label. "Me and ol' Buddy was lookin' for fun, out where the young girls go, Just cruisin' in circles on a Saturday night, doin' things that we loved so, Draggin' them cats and chasin' the chicks, and lookin' for the Hi-D-Ho."

41. "Looking Through Buddy's Eyes" by Sherry Holley. This 1992 curio from the Holley family (Larry's daughter) on "Cloud 9" Records did not have the desired effect of advancing Sherry's nascent country music career.

42. "Radio Slaves" by John Stewart. Country star Stewart referred to Buddy and Peggy Sue a couple of times in this compendium of '50s nostalgia, released on the Homecoming label in 1993: "Stratocasters, Fender amps, Buddy Holly and airplanes. The Great Pretender and fleeting fame. Elvis Presley, he was real, something that the girls could feel, something that the boys could steal."

43. "Buddy Holly Never Wrote a Song Called We're Too Punk" by Lawnmower Deth. We don't know much about this English band, who wrote and released this song in 1993 on their own Earache label, but we're dying to hear it.

44. "Buddy Holly" by Weezer. Not a tribute really, but rather a reference to the innocence of an earlier time, released on Geffen Records in 1995 and good enough to make the Top 10. The accompanying video used footage from the 1970s TV sitcom

Happy Days; Buddy himself did not appear.

45. "Buddy Holly" by Mike West. We don't know anything about this 1995 British record on the Quark label, but it's not the same song as Weezer's.

46. "Buddy Holly Said It All" by The Rick Thompson Band. This is the newest tribute, released in 1996 in the U.K. on JimRik Records. We'll second Rick's observation.

47. "Die Legend Von Buddy Holly" by Frank Rothe. We don't know when this song was released, on Holland's Electrola label.

Photo: Michael Ochs Archives

Nine

"I Feel Like An Actor In A Play, Who Doesn't Fit The Part"
Buddy Holly's Fictional Life

Though Buddy will probably never inspire an entire genre of fiction like Elvis Presley has, he does pop up now and again in literary fields of dreams.

Hawk and I stayed there for two days drinking beer, doing push-ups and watching cable television before Ives came with another guy to brief us. The other guy looked like Buddy Holly.

"As I'm sure you're aware," Buddy Holly said, "our agency has no authorization for internal matters, so this briefing is entirely informal and off the record." His heavy horn-rimmed glasses slipped down his thin nose a little and he pushed them back up with his left forefinger. He had a three-ring binder on the table in front of him....

"Where did you get this stuff?" I said, pointing with my chin toward Buddy Holly and his folder.

"The FBI supplies us with most of our domestic intelligence," Buddy Holly said.

"Sure," I said. A red Ford Bronco like Susan used to have came down the ramp from the bridge and turned left onto Main Street heading toward City Square. "We'll get them to help us."

Ives stood. "Punch in with us now and anon," he said. "We'll keep our nose right on the ground and feed you anything we catch."

I nodded. I could hear the click as Hawk poured himself some more wine. Buddy Holly closed his folder and slipped it into his briefcase and stood.

Ives opened the door. "Happy trails," he said. He went out.

Buddy Holly followed. "Glad to be able to help," he said. "Good luck."

"Sure," I said. "And it's a damned shame about you and the Big Bopper."

—*A Catskill Eagle* (Delacorte Press, 1985) by Robert B. Parker

"Eddie used his contacts. So did Wendell. They arranged for some people to come out and jam. Big people. You say Wendell called them kings? I guess they were. It was all secret. I mean *secret*. They never even acknowledged each other. You understand? No names. No introductions, no acknowledgements. They called each other Mr. Black and Mr. White, depending. No names, no pictures, nothing down on paper. They came to play, is all."

"Did they know they'd be taped?"

"Yeah. But everybody had veto power. They never had to use it though."

"Because Eddie died?"

"Not just Eddie. About everyone

who was there has died. The ones I recognized, at least. They weren't such a lucky bunch."

"Joann... who was there?"

"Eddie, Wendell... and... " She took a deep breath. "And Sam Cooke, for a night or two. Otis Redding. He stayed longer."

"Who were the Mr. Whites?

"Buddy Holly. Square-looking glasses and spit-curl. Some others I didn't know. It was some strange party."

—*Eddie and the Cruisers* (The Viking Press, 1980) by P.F. Kluge

Buddy shifted his Stratocaster and spoke.

"I don't know just how to say this." His words reverberated throughout Sky Vue with a calm power that made the Reverend's voice seem puny in retrospect. "I've been hearing a voice." He pointed upward.

The crowd murmured.

"It's been telling me things," Buddy said, pushing his glasses up with a forefinger. "Like how it might be decades or centuries before anyone comes to find me. Like how thirty years have already gone by as it is. Like how the world has changed, and how it wouldn't be home anymore."

The Bonanza passed over the theater, flying slowly. Buddy tilted his head to look at the silver object, and it was as if he were gazing at the airplane as well.

The object began to descend to him.

"So I'm taking this thing up on its offer," Buddy continued. "At first I couldn't decide, so I tossed a quarter. I'm going on tour." He unslung his Strat and lay it at his feet. "I'm told that I won't have a body while I'm gone and won't need one to make music, so I'll leave this one here. If anybody shows up before I do, you're welcome to use it. So long as you return it when I come back."

The silver object was so close now that its glow permeated his tousled hair.

Buddy grinned and nodded to us. "See you in the big time," he said.

—*Buddy Holly Is Alive and Well on Ganymede* (Avon Books, 1991) by Bradley Denton

"Dis is gon' be great," said Cordelia. She had slotted a cassette of Buddy Holley and the Crickets' greatest hits into the Blaupunkt player. The speaker system was far, far better than adequate.

"Cordelia," said Bagabond, "I like Buddy a lot, but maybe so he doesn't hurt my ears?"

"Oh, sorry," said Cordelia. She turned the volume knob down to barely endurable.

Then Saturday-evening traffic slowed to a stop-and-go creep within the tunnel, the stench of auto exhaust rose up in visible clouds, and the four in the Mercedes listened to all of Cordelia's Buddy Holley tapes before they reached New Jersey.

Cordelia had become more nervous the later it got. "Maybe there'll be a warm-up group," she'd muttered.

There hadn't been, but it turned out not to matter. When the four walked through the door of the Holidome lounge, they saw there was no need to worry about seats. Perhaps half the booths and tables were vacant. Clearly Saturday-night bacchanalia in New Brunswick didn't center here. They took a table about ten feet from the low stage, Jack and Bagabond on opposite sides, buffered by C.C. and Cordelia.

And Buddy Holley covered Prince.

Jack recognized Holley from the album portraits. He knew the musician was forty-nine, close enough to Jack's own age. Holley looked older. His face carried too much flesh; his belly wasn't completely camouflaged by the silver-lame jacket. He no longer wore the familiar old black horn-rims; his eyes were masked by stylish aviator shades that couldn't quite hide the dark bags. But he still played the Fender Telecaster like an angel.

The same couldn't be said for his sidemen. The rhythm guitarist and the bass player both looked about seventeen. Their playing was not inspired. The muddy sound mix didn't help. The drummer flailed at his snares, the volume coming through at about the right level to completely mask Holley's vocal delivery.

In rapid order Buddy Holley segued from Prince into a bad Billy Idol and then a so-so Bon Jovi.

"I don't believe it," said C.C., drinking a healthy dollop of her Campari and tonic. "All he's doing is covering top-forty shit."

Cordelia watched silently, her expression of initial enthusiasm visibly fading.

Bagabond shook her head disapprovingly. "We shouldn't have come."

Maybe, Jack thought, *he's biding his time*. "Give him a little while."

As the desultory clapping faded after a game attempt at evoking Ted Nugent, a voice from the back of the lounge yelled, "Come on, Buddy—give us some oldies!" A ragged cheer went up. Most of the clapping came from Cordelia's table.

Buddy Holley took his Telecaster by the neck and leaned toward the audience. "Well," he said, the West Texas twang still pronounced. "I don't usually take requests, but since you've been such a terrific crowd..." He settled back and strummed out a rapid-fire sequence of opening chords that his backup group more or less followed.

"Oh, lord," said C.C. She took another drink as Buddy Holley tore into Tommy Roe's "Hurray For Hazel," then a quick verse of "Sheila," finally a lugubrious, almost-bluesy version of Bobby Vinton's "Red Roses For a Blue Lady." Holley continued in that vein. He played a lot of music made famous by Bobbys and Tommys in the fifties and sixties.

"I want to hear 'Cindy Lou' or 'That'll Be the Day' or 'It's So Easy' or 'T-Town,' " said Cordelia, distractedly swirling her gin and tonic. "Not this shit."

I'll settle for "Not Fade Away," Jack thought. He watched Buddy Holley

slog through the dismal pop retrospective and started getting real depressed. It was enough to make him maybe wish that Holley had died at the height of his initial popularity and not survived to fall into this ghastly self-mockery.
—"The Second Coming of Buddy Holley," *Wild Cards Volume V: Down and Dirty* (Bantam Books, 1988) by Edward Bryant.

Buddy Holly plays his treasured Stratocaster in England.
Photo: Pictorial Press

Ten

"When Someday You'll Want Me, I'll Be There, Wait And See"
Buddy Holly's Currently Available CDs

Since 1983, MCA Records has been reissuing Buddy Holly's material by going back to the earliest, most pristine tapes available—preferably the first-generation studio tapes themselves. The use of these tapes has both a plus and minus side. The good news is that some of Buddy's recordings that were overdubbed after his death can now be heard the way Buddy himself recorded them. Also, many of his hits sound cleaner and brighter, and the four songs from his final recording session are available in stereo. The downside is that when new recordings are struck directly off the old studio tapes, without the equalization, compression and "signal boosting" that engineers employed to master the released versions in the 1950s, they don't sound as "tight" or as exciting as the originals. (Masters were generally made separately for 78-rpm records and 45-rpm singles. The ten-inch 78, originally designed for large players, could hold more bass. Seven-inch 45s were best suited for mid-range audio signals. Engineers compressed 45-rpm recordings, focusing on the mid-range in order to give the music more impact on small record players and radios.)

If you want to hear Buddy Holly the way his contemporaries heard him, you'll have to hunt down the singles and albums of that period. But generally the integrity of the recordings has been preserved on CD.

MCA has released the following albums on CD.

For the First Time Anywhere (MCAD 31048, 1983)—In early 1956 Buddy Holly, Jerry Allison, Don Guess and Sonny Curtis made a couple of trips to Norman Petty's studio in Clovis, New Mexico, to record six rockabilly demos for Decca Records, which had recently signed Buddy to a contract. The songs were **Rock-A-Bye Rock, Because I Love You, I'm Gonna Set My Foot Down, Changing All Those Changes, Baby Won't You Come Out Tonight** and **It's Not My Fault**. After Buddy's death, Petty overdubbed these recordings, as well as two other songs that Buddy had produced at the studio—**Bo Diddley** and Chuck Berry's **Brown-Eyed Handsome Man**—with an instrumental group called the Fireballs. The songs, released on a 1963 album called *Reminiscing*, were bitterly criticized by Hollyphiles because the Fireballs had obscured much of Holly's original recordings, and the more modern studio technology, tricked up to simulate stereo, sounded jarring against what had been done eight years earlier in mono. Also, the layering on of new overdubs meant that the final master was now at least a third or fourth generation tape, with the attendant hiss and loss of fidelity.

With *For the First Time Anywhere*, fans can hear these eight songs as Buddy had intended them to sound. The clarity has been improved immeasurably, and the full rawness of Buddy's rhythm section, particularly on the rockabilly songs, comes through loud and clear. These are great recordings.

To bring the package up to 10 tracks, MCA added two songs previously unavailable on U.S. albums: an early, loping **Maybe Baby** that lacked the excitement of the later, Little Richard-inspired hit version, and Buddy's shaky attempt at **That's My Desire**, a 1947 Frankie Laine classic, at his "Rave On" session in New York City. Though skimpy in length, *For the First Time Anywhere* at least put fans on notice that MCA would no longer slap together Buddy Holly packages with inferior tapes. The cover photo, bathed in orange light and showing Buddy without his glasses, was also used for the first time anywhere; it was an out-take from the photo session that produced the cover for his 1957 solo album.

From the Original Master Tapes

(MCAD-5540, 1985)—To replace all of MCA's former (and terrible) "best of Buddy Holly" albums, as well as to advertise the new company policy toward Buddy's music, executive Steve Hoffman gathered up the lost original tapes he'd found stashed in forgotten boxes on the Universal Studios backlot and assembled this album. From the 1956 Decca sessions there's **Rock Around With Ollie Vee**, first released on the B-side of a single in 1957. Then come the Crickets' charters: **That'll Be the Day, Oh, Boy!, Maybe Baby, It's So Easy** and **Think It Over**, along with three of their flipsides: **I'm Lookin' For Someone to Love, Not Fade Away** and **Tell Me How**. Buddy's solo A-sides (and a couple of Bs) are here as well: **Peggy Sue, Everyday, Words of Love, I'm Gonna Love You Too, Rave On, Well... All Right, Listen to Me, Heartbeat** and (in lush stereo) **It Doesn't Matter Anymore**. Rounding out the 20-song compilation is a crisp stereo version (complete with a snippet of studio chatter) of **True Love Ways**, a song that wasn't released until a year after Buddy's death, and **Reminiscing**, Buddy's 1958 collaboration with tenor saxophonist King Curtis; though neither song charted in the U.S., they were hits in Great Britain. The cover is a handsome, hand-tinted photo of Buddy taken at the "Rave On" session. There are no liner notes, but overall this is probably MCA's best Buddy Holly sampler for the general listener.

The Chirpin' Crickets (MCAD-

31182, 1987)—This is the second repackaging of Brunswick Records' 1958 *Chirpin' Crickets* album that many rock critics have called one of the greatest LPs of the rock 'n' roll era. (The first repackaging occurred in 1962, when Coral Records put a different photo on the front and retitled the album *Buddy Holly & the Crickets*.) This time around, MCA remastered the album from early-source tapes to make it sound as pristine as possible, and returned to the original cover photo that presented the Crickets as a quartet, rather than as Buddy Holly standing apart from three other guys; the photo also showcased Buddy's starburst Fender Stratocaster, which inspired a whole generation of rock guitarists.

The songs are among Holly's best: **Oh, Boy!**, **Not Fade Away**, **You've Got Love** (written in part by Roy Orbison), **Maybe Baby**, **It's Too Late** (written by Chuck Willis), **Tell Me How**, **That'll Be the Day**, **I'm Lookin' For Someone to Love**, **An Empty Cup** (another Roy Orbison song), **Send Me Some Lovin'** (a Little Richard ballad), **Last Night** and the underrated **Rock Me My Baby**. At a time when rock 'n' roll albums were loaded up with junky fillers, *The Chirpin' Crickets* had three hit recordings and nine other great ones. If there's any complaint about this album, it is only that Norman Petty overdubbed nine of the songs with a vocal group called the Picks, who often obfuscated Holly's vocals and guitar work. The overall sound quality here is good. (Released in Great Britain on Sequel NEMCD 629.)

Buddy Holly (MCAD 25239, 1987)—This is a reissue of the second album released during Buddy's lifetime, a solid compilation of his solo Coral records up to that time (early 1958), including the hit **Peggy Sue** and the soon-to-be-a-hit **Rave On**, plus **Words of Love, Mailman Bring Me No More Blues, Everyday, Listen to Me** and **I'm Gonna Love You Too**—in other words, both sides of Buddy's first three Coral singles are here. Rounding out the album are **Little Baby**, Fats Domino's **Valley of Tears** (made rather lugubrious by Norman Petty on organ), Elvis Presley's **(You're So Square) Baby I Don't Care**, Little Richard's **Ready Teddy**, and the one weak song in the bunch, **Look at Me**. (Released in Great Britain on Sequel NEMCD 630.)

The Buddy Holly Collection (MCAD2-10883, 1993)—Subtitled "50 Classic Recordings," this 2-CD package is MCA's attempt to bring together a wider spectrum of Buddy Holly's music by including obscurities with the better-known material. The result is sometimes less than satisfying. All 20 songs on the earlier *From the Original Master Tapes* are also here, so the purchase of this CD nullifies the buyer's need for that one. Among the remaining 30 songs, several are choice bits from *The Chirpin' Crickets* and *Buddy Holly* albums (**Ready Teddy, It's Too Late, Look at Me, Little Baby, You've Got Love, Rock Me My Baby** and **(You're So Square) Baby I Don't Care**)—in fact the only songs not available here from the *Buddy Holly* album are "Valley of Tears" and "Mailman Bring Me No More Blues" (which, frankly, is one of Buddy's most interesting recordings, considering that he recorded it extemporaneously after hearing a demo of the song); nine of the 12 cuts on *The Chirpin' Crickets* are also here, including an uncompressed **Maybe Baby** that sounds a little unfocused.

Buddy's 1956 Nashville period is represented by both sides of his first Decca single (**Blue Days, Black Nights** and **Love Me**), plus **Midnight Shift, Rock Around With Ollie Vee, Girl on My Mind, Ting-A-Ling** and **Modern Don Juan**. What distinguishes these remastered versions is the heavy presence of Don Guess's slap bass, which was less prominent when the recordings were released in the 1950s. There are also four early 1956 songs borrowed from the *For the First Time Anywhere* album. From the latter period of Buddy's life are his final singles: **Take Your Time** (the B-side of "Rave On"), **It's So Easy, Think It Over/Fool's Paradise, Early in the Morning, Heartbeat/ Well... All Right** and **It Doesn't Matter Anymore/Raining in My Heart** (both in stereo). The best of Buddy's studio demos, released after his death, are also included: **Reminiscing, Wishing, Love's Made a Fool of You** and the stereo **True Love Ways**.

Whoever picked the bookends for this 2-CD set really fell down on the job. The first three cuts are early demos made between late 1954 and early '56: **Down the Line** and **Soft Place in My Heart** (both of which are Buddy and Bob Montgomery duets) and an instrumental called **Holly Hop**. In the early '60s Norman Petty tried to hide the primitive condition of these recordings by overdubbing them with instrumental group the Fireballs; rather than go back to the original undubbed tapes here, MCA opted to use the clumsily overdubbed versions.

Petty's heavy-handed meddling is likewise evident when this compilation ends with four songs that Buddy recorded in his New York apartment in December '58 and January '59: **Peggy Sue Got Married, Crying, Waiting, Hoping, Learning the Game** and **What to Do**. Soon after Buddy's death, Coral Records got the tapes from his widow and overdubbed them with New York session musicians. "Peggy Sue Got Married"/"Crying, Waiting, Hoping" became Buddy's first posthumous single in 1959; all four songs appeared on *The Buddy Holly Story, Part 2* in 1960. Therefore, those early overdubs are the official versions that everybody heard at the time, and their arrangements became the blueprint for remakes by the Beatles, the Hullabaloos, the Searchers and others. In capping *The Buddy Holly Collection* with these four songs, MCA had the choice of (a) going with the familiar overdubbed versions or (b) using the intimate, rarely heard apartment tapes with just Buddy and his guitar. So what did MCA do? It (c) instead picked awkward stereo tapes that Norman Petty had created by overdubbing the Fireballs onto the bare tracks in the mid-1960s.

The accompanying booklet does a good job of covering Buddy's career, though thanks to an overzealous art director, the copy is sometimes illegible. Despite what the discography says, Buddy, not Sonny Curtis, played lead guitar on "Ting-A-Ling," and Ed "Dutch" McMillin, not Boots Randolph, blew sax on "Modern Don Juan." The cover photo, used originally on Buddy's 1965 *Showcase* album, makes him look like a prim schoolboy, not a rock 'n' roller.

Anyone wanting a comprehensive overview of Buddy's recording career will have to settle for this 50-song mini-box set for the time being. It ain't bad, but it could've been much better.

Buddy Holly's Greatest Hits

(MCAD-11213, 1995)—This latest, 18-song CD covers ground similar to *From the Original Master Tapes*, but has two less tracks. It includes **Early in the Morning, Fool's Paradise** and **Raining in My Heart**, which are not on the earlier CD, but drops **Tell Me How, Rock Around With Ollie Vee, Well... All Right, Listen to Me** and **Reminiscing**. The package is part of MCA's Ultimate MasterDisc gold series, in which the CD itself is handsomely plated with 24-karat gold and mastered from the original tapes. In his succinct overview of Buddy's life, booklet writer Mark Humphrey brings up an interesting point: Buddy and his sidemen cut the majority of their most well-known recordings while they were awaiting the release and subsequent chart-climbing of "That'll Be the Day"; afterward, the Crickets' frantic touring considerably slowed down their song production, until Buddy's career began to cool in late 1958. Somebody at MCA, however, should have corrected Mark's comments that "Words of Love" was released on Brunswick and that "Rave On" was a Crickets release. Our main complaint about this CD: Whoever mixed the stereo tracks—**It Doesn't Matter Anymore, Raining in My Heart** and **True Love Ways**—made no attempt to blend the channels and remove their uncomfortably wide separation.

Words of Love—Buddy Holly and the Crickets—28 Classic Tracks

(Polygram 514487-2, 1992)— Available only in the United Kingdom, this CD is a good presentation of Buddy Holly's music to both his fans and to a general audience. Blessed with a beautiful sepia-toned photo of Buddy live onstage at the London Palladium (probably the most dynamic cover of any Buddy Holly album ever released), *Words of Love* was advertised on national British TV. It reached the top of the album charts in early 1993, thirty-four years after Buddy's death. Since twice as many Buddy Holly songs charted in the U.K. as in the U.S., just about every track here qualifies as a hit, including the apartment tapes overdubbed by New York musicians and three tracks—**Bo Diddley, Brown-Eyed Handsome Man** and **Love Is Strange**—overdubbed by the Fireballs. Check the import shops for this one.

Buddy at Bell Sound, NYC, January 25, 1958 – singing "Rave On"
Photo: Bill Griggs Collection

Eleven

Bibliography

BOOKS

Amburn, Ellis, *Dark Star: The Roy Orbison Story*. New York: Carol Publishing Group, 1990
―――――, *Buddy Holly: A Biography*. New York: St. Martin's Press, 1995
Anderson, Christopher, *Jagger Unauthorized*. New York: Delacorte Press, 1993
Bashe, Philip, *Teenage Idol, Travelin' Man*. New York: Hyperion Books, 1992
Bean, J.P., *The Authorized Biography of Joe Cocker, With a Little Help From My Friends*. New York: Omnibus, 1990
Bryant, Edward; edited by George R.R. Martin, *Wild Cards V: Down and Dirty*, "The Second Coming of Buddy Holley." New York: Bantam Books, 1988
Clark, Dick and Richard Robinson, *Rock, Roll & Remember*. New York: Thomas Y. Crowell & Co., 1976
Clayson, Alan, *Only the Lonely*. New York: St. Martin's Press, 1989
Coleman, Ray, *Clapton*. New York: Warner Books, 1986
Crimp, Susan and Patricia Burstein, *The Many Lives of Elton John*. New York: Carol Publishing Group, 1992
Denton, Bradley, *Buddy Holly Is Alive and Well on Ganymede*, New York: William Morrow, 1991
DiMucci, Dion with Davin Seay, *The Wanderer*. New York: Beech Tree Books, 1988
Fox, Ted, *In the Groove*. New York: St. Martin's Press, 1986
Giuliano, Geoffrey, *Dark Horse: The Secret Life of George Harrison*. London: Bloomsbury Publ., 1989
Goldrosen, John, *Buddy Holly: His Life and Music*. Bowling Green, OH: Popular Press, 1975
Goldrosen, John & John Beecher, *Remembering Buddy*. London: Penguin Books, 1987
Griggs, Bill, *Buddy Holly: His Songs and Interviews (The Technical Stuff)*. Self-published, Lubbock, TX, 1995
Guralnick, Peter, *Lost Highway*. Boston: D.R. Godine Publishing, 1979
Haining, Peter, *Elvis In Private*. New York: St. Martin's Press, 1988
Holley, Larry, *The Buddy I Knew*. Self-published booklet, 1979
Karpp, Phyllis, *Ike's Boys*. Ann Arbor: Pierian Press, 1988
Kluge, P.F., *Eddie and the Cruisers*. New York: Viking Press, 1980
Laing, Dave, *Buddy Holly*. London: November Books, 1971
Minhinnett, Ray & Bob Young, *The Story of the Fender Stratocaster*. San Francisco; GPI Books, 1995
Parker, Robert B., *A Catskill Eagle*. New York: Delacorte Press, 1985
Peer, Elizabeth & Ralph II, *Buddy Holly... A Biography in Words, Photographs and Music*. Sydney, Australia: Peer International Corp., 1972

Roland, Tom, *The Billboard Book of Number One Country Hits*. New York: Billboard Books, 1991

Sanford, Christopher, *Mick Jagger*. London: Victor Gollancz, 1993

Schumacher, Michael, *Crossroads: The Life and Music of Eric Clapton*. New York: Hyperion, 1995

Selvin, Joel, *Rick Nelson: Idol For a Generation*. Chicago: Contemporary Books, 1990

Shelton, Robert, *No Direction Home*. New York: Beech Tree Books, 1986

Smith, Joe, *Off the Record—An Oral History of Popular Music*. New York: Warner Books, 1988

Thiele, Bob, as told to Bob Golden, *What a Wonderful World*. New York: Oxford University Press, 1995

Tobler, John and Stuart Grundy, *The Guitar Greats*. London: BBC Publications, 1983

Wale, Michael, *Vox Pop—Profiles of the Pop Process*. London: Harrap, 1972

Weinberg, Max, with Robert Santelli, *The Big Beat*. Chicago: Contemporary Books, 1984

Welch, Bruce, *Rock and Roll—I Gave You the Best Years of My Life*. London: Viking Books, 1989

White, Charles, *The Life and Times of Little Richard*. New York: Harmony Books, 1984

ARTICLES

Booe, Bob, "Bob Booe Remembers February 3, 1959," *Reminiscing*, Winter 1984

Booth, Dave and edited by Colin Escott, "The Everly Brothers," *Goldmine*, March 2, 1984

——————————, "Norman Petty: In the Studio With Buddy Holly," *Goldmine*, August 31, 1984

Bush, William J., "Buddy Holly: The Legend & Legacy," *Guitar Player*, June 1982

——————————, "Waylon Jennings Remembers Buddy Holly," *Guitar Player*, June 1982

Cajiao, Trevor, Jack Scott interview, *Now Dig This*, March 1989

——————————, "Sonny Curtis Talks About His New Album," *NDT*, December 1990

——————————, "Rocka-Billy Swan," *NDT*, August 1995

Roy Carr, "But Is It Cricket?" *New Musical Express*, September 24, 1977

Cauthen, Linda, "I'm Still in Love With Eddie Cochran!," *Sh-Boom*, June 1990

Clough, Brian, "Waylon Remembers," *NDT*, May 1989

Corbin, Larry, Waylon Jennings interview, *Reminiscing*, Winter 1982

Dawson, Jim, "Forget Reign of Buddy Holly? That'll Be the Day," *Denver Post*, June 30, 1974

——————————, "Buddy Holly, Pure & Simple," *Los Angeles Times*, November 28, 1982

——————————, "Norman Petty, The Genius Behind the Buddy Holly Sound," *Sh-Boom*, Oct/Nov 1990

——————————, Interviews with Steve Rash and Gary Busey, 1978

——————————, Interview with Snuff Garrett, 1980

——————————, Interview with Stevie Ray Vaughan, 1988

——————————, Interview with Ray Campi, October 3, 1995

Epstein, Dan, "The Oracle of Del-Fi," *Los Angeles Reader*, January 6, 1995

Fink, Stu, "Buddy Holly: Those Who Knew Him," *Goldmine*, July 18, 1986

Flans, Robyn, "Remember Buddy Holly (Again)," *Mix*, April 1996
Flippo, Chet, "The Buddy Holly Story," *Rolling Stone*, September 21, 1978
Floyd, Bill, Ted Scott interview, *Reminiscing*, Fall 1983
Griggs, Bill, Dr. Davis Armistead interview, *Reminiscing*, December 1981
———, Bill Pickering interview, *Reminiscing*, December 1981
———, Ben Hall interview, *Reminiscing*, March 1982
———, Jerry Allison interview, *Reminiscing*, June and September 1982
———, Gary Tollett interview, *Reminiscing*, Spring 1984
———, "Niki Sullivan: The Forgotten Cricket Remembers," *Goldmine*, August 31, 1984
———, Larry Welborn interview, *Reminiscing*, November 1986
———, Peggy Sue Rackham interview, *Reminiscing*, Feb/April/June 1988
———, Robert Linville interview, Clovis Music Festival program, August 1988
———, "The Buddy Holly Plane Crash: Accident or Murder?," *Sh-Boom*, Vol. 1, No. 1, 1989
Griggs, Bill and Jim O'Brien, "Cincinnati Rock and Rusty York," *Rockin' 50s*, June 1990
Goeppinger, Hans, "Don McLeod Remembers the Last Tour," *Reminiscing*, Winter 1984
Harris, Brandon, "The Norman Petty Chronicles," *Time Barrier*, April-May 1980
Harris, Paul, "Buddy's Buddies," *NDT*, October 1988
Holly, Buddy, Sophomore English assignment, 1953
Ingram, John, "George Atwood: Clowns, Jazz and Buddy Holly," *NDT*, January 1996
Jackson, Blair, "Buddy Holly's 'Not Fade Away,'" *Mix*, April 1996
Jones, Linda, "The Ballad of Buddy's Mom," *Buddy*, February 1974
Jones, Wayne, Interview with Carl Perkins, *Goldmine*, June 1980
———, Interview with Marshall Crenshaw, *Reminiscing*, Spring 1983
Krassner, Paul, "Jerry Garcia on Tour: The Way We Were," *Los Angeles Times*, August 20, 1995
Lennon, John, Letter to Jim Dawson, October 1974
Leigh, Spencer, "Words of Love: Memories of Buddy Holly," *NDT*, September and October, 1995
Mark, Norman, "The Life and Legend of 'This Unforgettable Texan,'" *Chicago Daily News Panorama*, April 15, 1967
Miller, Bill, "Collecting Buddy Holly," *Collecting*, December 1995
Miller, Jack, Niki Sullivan interview, *Reminiscing*, Spring 1984
Naylor, Bob & Trevor Cajiao, "Dream Dream Dream," *NDT*, July 1991
Newcombe, Jim, "Well It's a Darned Good Life and It's Kinda Funny," *NDT*, November 1987
Reif, Rita, "Auctions," *New York Times*, June 22, 1990
Riner, Bobette, "Buddy's Widow Talks," *Buddy*, June 1978
Sharp, Ken, "Buddy Holly Would Have Loved the Beatles," *Sh-Boom*, Oct/Nov 1990
Smith, Nigel & Damian Johnstone, Interview with Stan Rofe, *Reminiscing*, Spring 1983
Stafford, John, "The Robin Luke Story," *NDT*, July 1992

Stidom, Larry, "John Pickering & The Picks, Part 1" *Goldmine*, August 31, 1984
———, "John Pickering & The Picks, Part 2" *Goldmine*, September 14, 1984
Tamarkin, Jeff, "Skeeter Davis: They Just Don't Make 'Em Any Sweeter," *Goldmine*, January 31, 1986
Tobler, John, Interview with Carolyn Hester, *Folk Roots*, October 1993
Woodford, Chris, "The Wit and Wisdom of Jerry Lee Lewis," *NDT*, September 1995
"4500 Disc Fans Pack Troc—Despite Elvis," *Melody Maker*, March 8, 1958
"The Rock and Roll Hall of Fame," *Rolling Stone*, February 13, 1986
"That'll Be the Day, When You Say 'Good Buy!'," *People*, June 27, 1990

ALBUM LINER NOTES AND RECORDINGS
Buddy Holly, *The Complete Buddy Holly* (John Beecher and Malcolm Jones), MCA Coral CDSP 807, 1978
Ochs, Phil, *Gunfight at Carnegie Hall*, A&M SP-9010, 1974
Vee, Bobby, *I Remember Buddy Holly* (Bob Celii), EMI CDP-7 96057-2, 1992
Various Artists, *Not Fade Away*, Decca DRND-11260, 1996
Various Artists, *Texas Music Vol. 1*, Rhino R2 71781, 1994

RECORDED INTERVIEWS WITH BUDDY HOLLY
By Red Robinson backstage at the Georgia Auditorium, Vancouver, Canada, October 23, 1957
By Freeman Hoover at the Albany Hotel in Denver, Colorado, November 2, 1957
By Dale Lowry backstage at the Topeka Auditorium, Topeka, Kansas, November 5, 1957
By Pat Barton backstage at Newcastle Stadium, Newcastle, Australia, January 31, 1958
By Snuff Garrett at KSYD in Wichita Falls, Texas, in 1958
By Alan Freed on the *Big Beat* TV show, New York, September 23, 1958
By Dick Clark on *American Bandstand*, in Philadelphia, October 28, 1958
Other recordings
Taped phone call with Decca A&R man Paul Cohen, made from Jerry Allison's home, February 28, 1957

OTHER
The Howard Stern Show, January 3, 1996

Twelve

The Compilers

Jim Dawson is the author of several books, including *What Was the First Rock 'N' Roll Record?* (which *Mojo* magazine dubbed "one of the most impressive music reads of the year!"), *The Twist* and *Nervous Man Nervous: Big Jay McNeely and the Rise of the Honking Tenor Sax*. He has worked as an editor for *Hustler* and *Sh-Boom* magazines, and written for *Now Dig This*, *Goldmine* and the *Los Angeles Times*. Dawson can be reached at 1608 N. Cahuenga Blvd #442, Hollywood, CA 90028.

Spencer Leigh has written notes for over 100 CDs, including *The Best of Heartbeat*, which topped the U.K. album charts in 1994. He writes regularly for *Record Collector*, *Now Dig This* and *Country Music People*. His books include *Paul Simon—Now and Then*, *Speaking Words of Wisdom* (500 Quotes About the Beatles) and *Aspects of Elvis*. Leigh can be reached at his weekly radio programme, "On the Beat," at BBC Radio Merseyside, 55 Paradise Street, Liverpool L1 3BP, England.